Awaken My Heart

A LENT DEVOTIONAL

ALSO FROM DENISON FORUM

The Daily Article email newsletter is news discerned differently every Monday through Friday. Subscribe for free at DenisonForum.org.

Bold Faith

The Path To Purpose

The Fifth Great Awakening and the Future of America

How Does God See America?

What Are My Spiritual Gifts?

A Light Unto My Path: A Practical Guide to Studying the Bible

How to Bless God by Blessing Others: Words of Wisdom from the Early Church to Christians Today

Request these books and more at DenisonForum.org/store

© 2024 Denison Ministries

Scripture quotations are from the ESV® Bible (The Holy Bible, English Standard Version®), copyright © 2001 by Crossway, a publishing ministry of Good News Publishers. Used by permission. All rights reserved.

Scripture quotations marked (NIV) are taken from the Holy Bible, New International Version®, NIV®. Copyright © 1973, 1978, 1984, 2011 by Biblica, Inc.™ Used by permission of Zondervan. All rights reserved worldwide. www.zondervan.comThe "NIV" and "New International Version" are trademarks registered in the United States Patent and Trademark Office by Biblica, Inc.™

Awaken My Heart

A LENT DEVOTIONAL

Deepen your biblical insight through
Denison Forum Courses

In our first self-paced online course, *The Greatest Commandment*, you'll learn why Jesus linked loving God with loving others—and how you can better exercise each of those aspects of your faith.

This course includes five introductory videos from Dr. Jim Denison for each of its five sections, and each section includes five lessons. That's 25 lessons total. You may take the course at your own pace, or you may take it every weekday for 5 weeks.

The Greatest Commandment can be taken individually or within a small group as helpful reflection questions for each lesson are included.

Visit denisonforum.org/courses to begin today.

table of contents

WEEK 1: AWAKEN

- 10 Day 1: Join the Fifth Great Awakening
- 14 Day 2: "The garden of all the virtues"
- 18 Day 3: A flashlight in the dark
- 22 Day 4: One hour a week
- 26 Day 5: Public enemy No. 1

WEEK 2: BOW

- 32 Day 1: Live a life God can bless
- 36 Day 2: God deserves our worship
- 40 Day 3: Living in awe of God
- 44 Day 4: If you don't feel close to God
- 48 Day 5: Surrendering superiority
- 52 Day 6: The best advice I've ever received
- 56 Day 7: Reflection

WEEK 3: PRAY

- 60 Day 1: Prayer is the gate
- 64 Day 2: Persistent prayer
- 68 Day 3: My favorite prayer
- 72 Day 4: Confessing prayer
- 76 Day 5: Knocking on God's door at midnight
- 80 Day 6: Drawing on God's bank account
- 84 Day 7: Reflection

WEEK 4: SEEK

- 88 Day 1: You were made for a purpose
- 92 Day 2: With all your heart
- 96 Day 3: God is not a hobby
- 100 Day 4: Praying like Abraham Lincoln
- 104 Day 5: A door with no handle
- 108 Day 6: Entering a sterile room
- 112 Day 7: Reflection

WEEK 5: TURN

- 116 Day 1: I am directionally challenged
- 120 Day 2: Jesus' most surprising apostle
- 124 Day 3: Crucified upside down
- 128 Day 4: A sermon I've never forgotten
- 132 Day 5: Praying for "the gift of tears"
- 136 Day 6: "Create in me a clean heart"
- 140 Day 7: Reflection

WEEK 6: TRUST

- 144 Day 1: The resolution your heart wants to make
- 148 Day 2: When you can't trace his hand, trust his heart
- 152 Day 3: God redeems all he allows
- 156 Day 4: "All of God there is, is in this moment"
- 160 Day 5: Eighteen inches from God
- 164 Day 6: Your spiritual alarm clock

WEEK 7: PREPARE (HOLY WEEK)

- 170 Day 1 (Palm Sunday): Don't join the crowd
- 174 Day 2: You are God's temple
- 178 Day 3: Are you in love with God?
- 182 Day 4: Sitting at the feet of God
- 186 Day 5 (Maundy Thursday): When you question God's love for you
- 190 Day 6 (Good Friday): Why did Jesus have to die for you?
- 194 Day 7: Grace is greater than guilt
- 198 Day 8 (Easter Sunday): Join the "Fellowship of the Unashamed"

INTRODUCTION

Lent is among the oldest of Christian traditions still practiced today. It traces its origins back to the first generations of the church, but the practice was formalized at the First Council of Nicaea in 325 AD. Lent's original purpose was to help new believers prepare for baptism, but it soon grew beyond that to become a time of penance and preparation for all believers in the weeks leading up to Easter.

However, for many of us, Lent may be a relatively foreign practice, an unnecessary burden performed for ritual rather than spiritual reasons. To be sure, there are those who go to church on Ash Wednesday and fast from something they enjoy because it's simply what you do during this time of year.

But it doesn't have to be that way.

Lent can still serve its ancient purpose of uniting God's people across all walks of life and denominations of the faith in reflecting on Christ's life, message, and sacrifice. To that end, over the course of the next seven weeks and culminating on Easter Sunday, we're going to ask God to awaken the hearts of our nation, our culture, and ultimately ourselves to the truth of his word and the necessity of a consistent walk with him.

This guide is designed to be read daily, starting on Ash Wednesday and ending on Easter Sunday, though the lessons included are relevant for any time of the year. Each entry will require only a few minutes to read, but our hope is that the suggested reflections, questions, and prayer topics will spur you to spend much longer in conversation with the Father about what you've learned and experienced through that day's devotional.

May you draw closer to the Lord over the forty-seven days of this Lenten devotional, joining the millions of Christians around the globe who are likewise seeking God as we approach the celebration of Easter.

WEEK ONE

Awaken

ASH WEDNESDAY

Join the Fifth Great Awakening

—

"If my people who are called by my name humble themselves, and pray and seek my face and turn from their wicked ways, then I will hear from heaven and will forgive their sin and heal their land." —2 Chronicles 7:14

DAY 1

I've often heard people pray for God to bring revival to our nation, yet rarely have I heard prayers for a great awakening. But throughout its history, the Western world has actually seen four "great awakenings." What's the difference, you may ask?

Revivals change people and churches. Awakenings change cultures and nations.

The First Great Awakening is dated to 1734 under the preaching of pastor and theologian Jonathan Edwards and the British evangelist George Whitefield. Before it began, only 5 percent of colonial Americans identified with a Christian church. At its height, 80 percent were active followers of Jesus.

The Second Great Awakening is dated to 1792 and was sparked by a prayer movement led by a Baptist minister named Isaac Backus. This movement led to more than a thousand large gatherings, called camp meetings, being held across the country. Churches doubled and tripled in membership, and William Carey began what we now consider the modern missions movement.

The Third Great Awakening is dated to 1858, resulting from a "businessman's prayer meeting" movement that began the previous year in New York City. Out of a national population of thirty million people, more than a million came to Christ in a single year. And at one point, fifty thousand were turning to Jesus for salvation every week. This revival continued into the Civil War, when more than one hundred thousand soldiers were converted.

And the Fourth Great Awakening began in Wales in 1904. This awakening impacted every sphere of culture and industry. Police formed barbershop quartets to sing in churches since there was no one to arrest. Saloons went bankrupt. Coal mines even shut down briefly because the miners became converted, stopped using obscene language, and the mules could no longer understand their commands. This awakening spread to the US: for example, out of fifty thousand residents in Atlantic City, New Jersey, only fifty were unconverted. Two hundred stores in Portland, Oregon, closed every day so people could attend prayer meetings.

Now the world is seeing a Fifth Great Awakening.

China's underground church is exploding in growth. Churches are growing exponentially in Cuba and across Latin and South America. And sub-Saharan Africa is witnessing a remarkable advance of the gospel.

Will we see this awakening in America? Is an awakening of this magnitude even possible today?

We believe it is, but it has to start with us. So, what would that look like?

Notes

God's promise is clear in today's verse:

- We must humble ourselves, admitting we need the transforming movement of God's Spirit.

- Then we must "pray." The original word in Hebrew means to pray passionately and collectively.

- God says we must seek his face, which in Hebrew means to "run hard after" personal intimacy with the Lord.

- And when we do, we must "turn from our wicked ways" as his Spirit reveals them to us.

If we will, our Father promises to hear us, forgive us, and heal our land.

GUIDED PRAYER

1. Meditate on God's gracious desire to "heal our land."

- "Blessed is the nation whose God is the LORD" (Psalm 33:12).

2. Pray for the Lord to bring the Fifth Great Awakening to our land. Would you commit to intercede daily for a movement of God in our nation and our world?

- "Ask, and it will be given to you; seek, and you will find; knock, and it will be opened to you" (Matthew 7:7).

3. Ask God to show you ways to participate in his plan for spiritual renewal, then commit yourself to joining his Spirit at work each day.

- "As each has received a gift, use it to serve one another, as good stewards of God's varied grace" (1 Peter 4:10).

GO

James 4:8 promises: "Draw near to God, and he will draw near to you." I can think of no better time to accept his invitation and pray for others to do the same than Lent: a season when God's people from across every denomination are reflecting on his life, message, and sacrifice.

So let's close this day with a practical way to accept his invitation as well as share it with others.

Rodney "Gypsy" Smith (1860–1947) conducted evangelistic campaigns in the US and Great Britain across seven decades. He was once asked how revival begins. His answer: "Go home, lock yourself in your room. Kneel down in the middle of the floor, and with a piece of chalk, draw a circle around yourself. There, on your knees, pray fervently and brokenly that God would start a revival within that chalk circle."

Will you draw such a circle around your soul today?

Will you invite others to do the same tomorrow?

Extended reading: Acts 2

THURSDAY

"The garden of all the virtues"

—

"By the grace given to me I say to everyone among you not to think of himself more highly than he ought to think, but to think with sober judgment, each according to the measure of faith that God has assigned." —Romans 12:3

DAY 2

I have struggled with understanding humility my entire Christian life.

My problem is not so much with *appearing* to be humble. Like most people, I have learned over the years to deflect praise and to act in self-deprecating ways that hopefully convince others of my humility. Nor is my problem with *wanting* to be humble. I genuinely do want to be a person of humility with God, others, and myself.

My problem is with truly *being* humble in my own inner thoughts and feelings.

I've realized over time that this is because I picked up the wrong idea of humility along the way. I thought that to be genuinely humble meant to think less of myself than

I would otherwise, to devalue my gifts, abilities, and accomplishments. But this felt less than honest. My gifts, abilities, and accomplishments are real. So are yours.

But if we recognize them for what they are, how is this humility?

It turns out, I needed to change my definition of humility from thinking less of myself to thinking of myself less (as Rick Warren noted in *The Purpose Driven Life*). I needed to shift my focus from myself to my Lord, recognizing that my gifts and abilities do not come from my own achievement but from his grace.

This is what it means to "think with sober judgment," as our verse today suggests. When we admit that our abilities come from our Creator and not ourselves, we will not think of ourselves "more highly than [we] ought to think." We will turn our attention from ourselves to our Lord. From pride to gratitude. And genuine humility will be the result.

Think about this with me for a moment: Did you earn the right to be born? Did you do something to produce your life? Did you deserve to be "born again" (John 3:3)? Did you meet a list of requirements that produced your eternal life?

What about your gifts and abilities? Were those acquired or given? Did you earn every opportunity of education and experience that has come your way? Do any of us have even a little control over the air we are breathing right now?

The life we are living is a gift.

St. John Chrysostom (AD 347–407) observed, "Humility is the garden of all the virtues."

May God foster in us a healthy garden for his fruit to grow as we spend time in prayer.

Notes

GUIDED PRAYER

1. Reflect on the gifts and abilities that enable you to live your life and do your work. Think about how each of them finds its source not in your merit but in your Father's grace.

- "Never be wise in your own sight" (Romans 12:16).

2. Respond to his grace with gratitude and humility.

- "Let not the wise man boast in his wisdom, let not the mighty man boast in his might, let not the rich man boast in his riches, but let him who boasts boast in this, that he understands and knows me, that I am the Lord who practices steadfast love, justice, and righteousness in the earth" (Jeremiah 9:23–24).

3. Choose to use your gifts and abilities to honor your Creator and to serve everyone he loves.

- "If you pour yourself out for the hungry and satisfy the desire of the afflicted, then shall your light rise in the darkness and your gloom be as the noonday" (Isaiah 58:10).

GO

Every gift, ability, and opportunity in your life is to be used to love your Lord and your neighbor. And serving our neighbor is often our best way of serving our Father.

John Wesley observed, "One of the principal rules of religion is to lose no occasion of serving God. And since he is invisible to our eyes, we are to serve him in our neighbor, which he receives as if done to himself in person, standing visibly before us."

May our love for God be evident today as we generously serve those around us with a heart of humility.

Extended reading: Luke 15:11–32

"By the grace given to me I say to everyone among you not to think of himself more highly than he ought to think, but to think with sober judgment, each according to the measure of faith that God has assigned."

ROMANS 12:3

FRIDAY

A flashlight in the dark

—

"This is the confidence that we have toward him, that if we ask anything according to his will he hears us." —1 John 5:14

DAY 3

The most frequent question I've been asked over nearly fifty years of ministry is, "How can I know God's will for my life?"

It's a commendable and extremely practical question.

We should all want to live a life God can bless. We know that God can't bless what's not in his will, which would amount to rewarding sin and encouraging what harms his children. But finding his will can feel so abstract, a mystery we must struggle to unravel, a map we must try to decode.

As a college freshman, I was struggling with this issue, trying to make decisions regarding my major and already thinking about my next steps after graduation. I was talking with one of our religion professors, a wise mentor who became a spiritual father to me over the years.

He smiled and said, "God's will is not a searchlight that reveals your final destination but a flashlight that shows you the next step on the journey."

This image has stayed with me ever since.

No one in the Bible gets a "five-year plan." Paul thought he was supposed to go east when he was called west (Acts 16:6–10). When he followed God's Macedonian call, he did not know he was introducing the word of God to what we call "Europe" today. He did not know that European Christians would take the gospel farther west into the New World one day. He couldn't know that, centuries later, I would be writing this devotional as a result.

Yet praying in God's will is vital to praying effectively. No good father will give his children something that would harm them. When we "ask anything according to his will," we can know that "he hears us" and will give us what is best in response (1 John 5:14).

So make it your resolution every day to live and pray in the will of God. Start your day by meeting with the Lord, surrendering your day to his Spirit's leading and empowering. Ask him to guide you each step of the way as each step comes. Ask yourself what Scripture says about the decisions you face and choose to live biblically.

Listen for the Spirit's voice in your spirit. Ask your Father to open and close doors according to his purpose for you. Make it your ambition to live and pray in his will and he will help you.

The bottom line is simple: God wants us to know his will more than we want to know it. If we truly want to live and pray in his will, we will.

Notes

GUIDED PRAYER

1. Meditate on your Father's perfect will. Consider his omniscience and his love for you, and reflect on the fact that he can only want what is best for you.

- "Do not be conformed to this world, but be transformed by the renewal of your mind, that by testing you may discern what is the will of God, what is good and acceptable and perfect" (Romans 12:2).

2. Choose to live by God's word, remembering that his word will never contradict his will.

- "Your word is a lamp to my feet and a light to my path. I have sworn an oath and confirmed it, to keep your righteous rules" (Psalm 119:105–106).

3. Listen for his voice in your spirit. Ask that he would help you walk through your day today in his presence and purpose.

- "Trust in the LORD with all your heart, and do not lean on your own understanding. In all your ways acknowledge him, and he will make straight your paths" (Proverbs 3:5–6).

GO

My college professor made a lifelong contribution to my life and ministry when he helped me understand God's will better. Helping other people in this way is a great gift to them and to everyone they influence.

Alfred North Whitehead suggested that great people plant trees they'll never sit under. When you help someone live and pray in God's will, you are planting such trees that will bear harvest for eternity.

Would you ask the Lord to help you give a gift like that today?

Extended reading: Acts 16:6–40

"This is the confidence that we have toward him, that if we ask anything according to his will he hears us."

1 JOHN 5:14

SATURDAY

One hour a week

—

"Seek the L<small>ORD</small> and his strength; seek his presence continually!" —1 Chronicles 16:11

DAY 4

Imagine spending one hour a week with your family. How strong would your family be? Now, if you are employed, imagine working one hour a week. How strong would your income be?

Or imagine focusing on your health for just an hour a week, then consuming anything else you want the rest of the week. How strong would your body be?

This is what happens to our souls when we separate Sunday from Monday and the "spiritual" from the "secular." It's what happens when we focus on religion only when we are at church on Sunday morning and occasionally during the week (even with devotionals like this one).

God can only lead us where we'll follow and can only give what we're willing to receive. When we "seek his presence continually," as our verse calls for, we experience his presence continually. We experience the leadership of his omniscience, the provision of his omnipotence, and the blessing of his unconditional love.

This is one reason our Enemy partners with our secular culture to compartmentalize our lives. Even going back to the ancient Greco-Roman world, we have been taught that religion is a transaction with God or gods. Place a sacrifice on their altar so they will bless your crops, or protect you in war, or do whatever else you want them to do.

People in that day did not want a personal, intimate relationship with the gods atop Mount Olympus. They did what the gods required so the gods would do what they required.

Christianity is completely different: it is about a full-time, unconditional relationship with our Maker. It is about seeking God's constant presence in prayer, Bible study, worship, and other spiritual disciplines. It is about knowing Christ and then making him known as the focus and purpose of our lives. We spend time in God's presence not to earn his love and favor but because we already have it.

Part-time discipleship is a contradiction. It is like being partly pregnant or partly a parent. You either are or you are not.

Let's respond to today's verse by seeking "the Lord and his strength" and seeking his presence "continually." Let nothing stand between you and a full-time, unconditional commitment to your Lord.

Timothy Keller was right when he wrote this in *The Meaning of Marriage*: "To be loved but not known is comforting but superficial. To be known and not loved is our greatest fear. But to be fully known and truly loved is, well, a lot like being loved by God. It is what we need more than anything. It liberates us from pretense, humbles us out of our self-righteousness, and fortifies us for any difficulty life can throw at us."

You can experience a love like that with your Father today. Connect with him as we spend time in guided prayer.

GUIDED PRAYER

1. Reflect on God's unconditional, passionate love for you.

- "See what kind of love the Father has given to us, that we should be called children of God; and so we are" (1 John 3:1).

2. Ask the Spirit to show you areas of your life that are separated from your Lord. Have you divided your week into spiritual versus secular, religion versus the real world? Is there any area of your life that you need to surrender to him today?

- "If then you have been raised with Christ, seek the things that are above, where Christ is, seated at the right hand of God. Set your minds on things that are above, not on things that are on earth" (Colossians 3:1–2).

3. Take your next step into full-time, unconditional communion with your Father.

- "One thing I have asked of the Lord, that will I seek after: that I may dwell in the house of the Lord all the days of my life, to gaze upon the beauty of the Lord and to inquire in his temple" (Psalm 27:4).

GO

We live in a secular society that has attempted to privatize religion, insisting that we keep our beliefs to ourselves so that we don't offend others with what they view as "intolerance." This conflict explains much of the chaos and angst of our day. God cannot bless those who will not admit they need his blessing. He can only heal those who want his healing.

Pray today for the Lord to use your unconditional commitment to him as an example for others. Invite those you influence to take their next step into such transformation. And know that you are acting as a catalyst for the spiritual awakening we need so desperately today.

Extended reading: Psalm 91

"Seek the Lord and his strength; seek his presence continually!"

1 CHRONICLES 16:11

SUNDAY

Public enemy No. 1

—

"Today salvation has come to this house, since he is a son of Abraham. For the Son of Man came to seek and to save the lost." —Luke 19:9–10

DAY 5

Zacchaeus was one of the wealthiest men in the Gospels. And perhaps the most despised by his neighbors. Tax collectors occupied the most hated profession in Jesus' society. Such people were hated and rejected by their fellow Jews. And the more tax collectors extorted from their victims, the more hated they became.

Enter Zacchaeus, the "chief tax collector" of Jericho, who we find in Luke 19:2. This title isn't found anywhere else in the literature of the day and explains why Luke describes him as "rich." As a "chief" tax collector, Zacchaeus organized the other tax collectors in the region and took a cut from their labor.

And Zacchaeus worked in Jericho, one of the most lucrative places for tax collecting in all of Israel. As the most significant city on the major east-west road between Judea and Perea, it saw travelers from across that part of the world. This provided the perfect environment for Zacchaeus and the other tax collectors under his leadership to take advantage of those passing through.

Now Jesus has come to town and has called this notorious man by name (v. 5). Everyone there must have been wondering: Would he condemn Zacchaeus for his corruption? Would he challenge him and his employees to repent of their many sins?

Shocking everyone who heard him—probably Zacchaeus most of all— Jesus said, "I must stay at your house today" (v. 5). Unsurprisingly, the crowd "grumbled" and complained, "He has gone to be the guest of a man who is a sinner" (v. 7).

But Zacchaeus himself responded differently. He received him joyfully and later announced, "Behold, Lord, the half of my goods I give to the poor. And if I have defrauded anyone of anything, I restore it fourfold" (v. 8). His "goods" referred to everything he owned, not just his income as a chief tax collector. And by restoring the money he defrauded by "fourfold" he was fulfilling the requirements of the Law found in Exodus 22:1 and the prophets in 2 Samuel 12:6.

And in Luke 19:9–10, Jesus replied, "Today salvation has come to this house, since he also is a son of Abraham." He then added, "The Son of Man came to seek and to save the lost."

As we reflect on God's call for his people to "turn from their wicked ways," Zacchaeus reminds us that genuine turning from sin must produce practical results in our lives. When we turn from our ways, we live differently. When we are forgiven, we must forgive others. When we are made right with our Lord, we must seek to be right with our neighbors.

Is your repentance changing how you live? When last did repentance cost you something significant?

Let's ask God to show us how to respond like Zacchaeus today as we enter a time of guided prayer.

GUIDED PRAYER

1. Imagine yourself as Zacchaeus watching Jesus come into town. Hear him call your name and invite himself to your home. Feel his surprise at God's astounding grace.

- "From his fullness we have all received, grace upon grace" (John 1:16).

2. Ask the Spirit to show you ways that Zacchaeus' story is your story today. Confess anything you need to admit to your Father and receive his unconditional love.

- "Let us then with confidence draw near to the throne of grace, that we may receive mercy and find grace to help in time of need" (Hebrews 4:16).

3. Ask the Lord to show you how to live out your repentance in the way you love and serve others today.

- "As each has received a gift, use it to serve one another, as good stewards of God's varied grace" (1 Peter 4:10).

GO

Charles Spurgeon observed, "Another proof of the conquest of a soul for Christ will be found in a real change of life. If a man does not live differently from what he did before, both at home and abroad, his repentance needs to be repented of and his conversion is a fiction."

If a person truly encounters God's forgiving love, he must "live differently from what he did before." Will those who know you say you have experienced that grace today?

Extended reading: Luke 15

"Today salvation has come to this house, since he is a son of Abraham. For the Son of Man came to seek and to save the lost."

LUKE 19:9-10

WEEK TWO

Bow

MONDAY

Live a life God can bless

—

"Blessed are the poor in spirit, for theirs is the kingdom of heaven." —Matthew 5:3

DAY 1

My wife is one of the most godly, practical people I have ever had the pleasure of knowing. She has taught women's Bible studies for nearly forty years and has several wise sayings she is well-known for.

For example, when our sons were growing up, she often encouraged them to "live a life that God can bless." She was right: experiencing the blessing of an all-knowing and all-powerful God is the key to our best lives.

But how do we do this?

Last week we explored God's promise to "heal our land" if his people "humble themselves, and pray and seek my face and turn from their wicked ways" (2 Chronicles 7:14). This week, we'll focus on the first of these imperatives: *humility*.

Our verse for today comes from Jesus' first beatitude, or path to blessing, found in Matthew 5:3: "Blessed are the poor in spirit, for theirs is the kingdom of heaven." The word *blessed* is a translation of the original Greek word *makarios*, which refers to a deep inner joy that nothing in life can give or steal. By contrast, "poor" in our verse does not mean poverty (*penes*) but instead describes absolute destitution (*ptochos*). It means a person who has no food, clothes, or possessions of any kind.

The phrase "in spirit" shows the kind of poverty Jesus means. To be "poor in spirit" is to recognize our spiritual bankruptcy before God. The New English Bible translates this phrase well: "Blessed are those who know their need of God."

Why? "For theirs is the kingdom of heaven."

"The kingdom of heaven" is the place where God rules as king. In Matthew 6:10, Jesus taught us to pray, "Your kingdom come, your will be done, on earth as it is in heaven." Here's the problem: We will only make God our king when we know how much we need him. Otherwise, we'll attempt to be king instead.

It's here we discover the foundational question for all genuine success, joy, peace, and happiness in life: *Who is your king: you or God?*

Being poor in spirit starts with admitting that we don't know how to live our lives or make our own decisions, so we always pray first. We put God in charge of our problems and ambitions, our struggles and our dreams.

When we are poor in spirit, we recognize every day that life is not about us. What truly matters is living in a way that glorifies Jesus and invites the people around us to make him their king. It's understandable that people would judge Christ by Christians. When we live in ways that honor our Lord, we lead others to honor him as well.

Notes

Everything we do is a means to this end.

So here's the question: Are you "poor in spirit"? Have you been living your life with God as king, or have you been trying to take control yourself?

If you're not sure, think about it in these ways.

When was the last time you surrendered an important decision to him?

What was the last problem you entrusted to him in prayer?

What about the last time you surrendered your will and chose his, even though you may not have understood or agreed?

And if you were to ask him, would God say he is your king today?

If not, know that God isn't looking at you with frustration and disappointment. Rather, he's inviting you today to recognize that he loves you more than you can comprehend and desires to see you live a life full of blessing and joy.

Will you let him be your good king today?

GUIDED PRAYER

1. Meditate on the difference God makes when he is king of our lives.

- "Seek first the kingdom of God and his righteousness, and all these things will be added to you" (Matthew 6:33).

2. Ask the Spirit to show you any area of your life where you are not "poor in spirit" but living as the king of your life and world.

- "Humble yourselves, therefore, under the mighty hand of God so that at the proper time he may exalt you" (1 Peter 5:6).

3. Decide to make God your king in every area of your life.

Ask him to help you trust that he can do more with your life than you can on your own.

- "Whoever humbles himself like this child is the greatest in the kingdom of heaven" (Matthew 18:4).

GO

A surgeon can only help patients who humble themselves enough to admit they cannot heal themselves. As we go today, let us walk in humility as well, admitting our need for God and submitting our lives to him.

When we are "poor in spirit," Jesus promises that we will be "blessed."

Will you live a life that God can bless today?

Will you help someone else do the same?

Extended reading: Micah 6

TUESDAY

God deserves our wörship

—

*"Humble yourself before the
Lord, and he will exalt you."*
—James 4:10

DAY 2

Have you ever wondered why God insists that we seek to glorify him?

His word is clear: "My glory I will not give to another" (Isaiah 48:11). He created us for his glory (Isaiah 43:7) and calls us to "let your light shine before others, so that they may see your good works *and glorify your Father who is in heaven*" (Matthew 5:16, my emphasis). Even Paul commanded us in 1 Corinthians 10:31, "Whether you eat or drink, or whatever you do, do all to the glory of God."

If anyone else made such a requirement, we would consider them to be extremely prideful, an attention seeker, and certainly the opposite of the humility we're focusing on this week.

But there are two reasons why God seeks his own glory so emphatically.

The first reason is that to glorify anyone before God himself would be to commit idolatry.

Let me explain in this way: If God allowed us to worship and serve anyone before himself, he would be encouraging us to invest our hearts and lives into meaningless and powerless substitutes. Idols are neither worthy of worship nor beneficial to us or the world. God alone is worthy of that glory.

That's why the first of the Ten Commandments is foundational to all the rest: "You shall have no other gods before me" (Exodus 20:3). It is only in worshiping the true God that we don't waste our worship.

The second reason is that humility before God enables us to experience the fruit of his grace in our lives.

It helps us remember that we are the creation before our Creator, children before our Father, patients before our Great Physician, sheep before our Good Shepherd.

Pride, by contrast, turns us from this beautiful relationship with our provider and protector and instead focuses us on ourselves in all our fallen, broken sinfulness. And instead of living as his children, we attempt to be the parent, the boss. If you've ever seen this dynamic play out in real life, you know that this rarely works out well. God is the one in charge, and so this old saying still rings true today: "To get along with God, stay off his throne."

Now this may sound stern or challenging, but our Lord calls us to humility because he loves us and wants only the best for us. And he knows that his best far exceeds our best. Our verse for today reminds us of this truth: "Humble yourself before the Lord, and he will exalt you" (James 4:10). Our Father *wants* to "exalt" his children, but he cannot do so until we humble ourselves before him.

Notes

Otherwise, as we have seen, he would be permitting things that can only harm us.

But when we humble ourselves before him, seeking to be made more like Jesus, we experience this amazing fact from Romans 8:30, "Those whom he predestined he also called, and those whom he called he also justified, and those whom he justified he also glorified."

And Jesus' prayer for his followers in John 17:22 becomes our experience: "The glory that you have given me I have given to them, that they may be one even as we are one."

So as counterintuitive as it may feel, our own joy, peace, hope, and, yes, glory don't come from lifting ourselves up but instead by humbling ourselves before our worthy God.

Would you humble yourself today before your glorious Lord?

He deserves your worship, and you will experience his best in response.

GUIDED PRAYER

1. Meditate on the fruit that comes from a life of humility before God.

- "Whoever exalts himself will be humbled, and whoever humbles himself will be exalted" (Matthew 23:12).

2. Ask the Spirit to show you any idols in your life, any people or priorities which are taking precedence over the Lord.

- "Little children, keep yourselves from idols" (1 John 5:21).

3. Choose to humble yourself before God today.

Spend time reading a psalm of praise to him, such as Psalm 100. Sing a hymn or chorus of praise. The more we exalt God, the more humble we become.

- "I will bless the LORD at all times; his praise shall continually be in my mouth" (Psalm 34:1).

GO

The path to humility can be a challenging one. Just when you become certain you are a humble person, you may, in fact, be the opposite. Taking pride in our humility is a contradiction in terms.

Instead, each day we need to ask the Lord to reveal areas of pride in our lives, then repent and seek to glorify him once again. This is a continual process of humility that begins with our relationship toward God and then extends to our relationships with others as well.

Proverbs 15:33 puts it this way, "Humility comes before honor." When we seek God's honor before our own, we will be honored in return. But if we seek to honor God so that we'll be honored, we're not truly honoring God in the first place.

Rick Warren had it right when he said: "Humility is not thinking less of yourself; it is thinking of yourself less." Let us walk in that humility in our relationships with God and others today.

Extended reading: Psalm 145

WEDNESDAY

Living in awe of God

—

*"Woe is me! For I am lost; for I am a man of unclean lips, and I dwell in the midst of a people of unclean lips; for my eyes have seen the King, the L*ord *of hosts!" —Isaiah 6:5*

DAY 3

I will never forget the evening I met Billy Graham.

I was part of a group chosen to invite him to lead an outreach event in the Dallas-Fort Worth area. He was preaching on a college campus in California at the time so our group met with him in a locker room beneath the stadium.

Before our meeting, I put more thought than usual into what I would wear and what I would say. I thoroughly prepared for our conversation and wanted to be very intentional with everything I said and did.

Thankfully, Dr. Graham could not have been more gracious and humble with our group. And even though I came with a well-prepared plan to present to him, I found myself in awe just to be in his presence. Yet Billy ultimately was just a man, albeit an amazing man of God.

But if I experienced this level of awe for Billy Graham, how much more awe should I be experiencing for God himself?

So as we continue our weeklong focus on humility, consider what these stories from Scripture have in common:

- When "the Lord appeared to Abram" (Genesis 17:1), "Abram fell on his face" (v. 3).

- When Moses met God at the burning bush, Moses "hid his face, for he was afraid to look at God" (Exodus 3:6).

- When Jeremiah heard God's call to serve as his prophet, he responded, "Ah, Lord God! Behold, I do not know how to speak, for I am only a youth" (Jeremiah 1:6).

- When Jesus demonstrated his omnipotence on the Sea of Galilee, Peter "fell down at Jesus' knees, saying, 'Depart from me, for I am a sinful man, O Lord'" (Luke 5:8).

- When John met the risen Christ on the prison island of Patmos, he testified: "When I saw him, I fell at his feet as though dead" (Revelation 1:17).

In our famous text from Isaiah 6, the prophet Isaiah "saw the Lord sitting upon a throne" (v. 1). In light of God's holiness, he recognized and admitted his own sinfulness. Then a seraphim, which is a heavenly being, took a burning coal from the altar, touched Isaiah's mouth, and cleansed his sin (vv. 2–7). In response to such grace, Isaiah accepted God's call (v. 8) and became one of the greatest prophets in human history.

Thankfully, God is not asking us to use burning coals. But to experience true and transforming humility, we must see God as he is before we can see ourselves as we truly are. As long as you are judging or comparing yourself to other people, you will always be able to find someone to whom you feel superior. And if you are judging yourself by yourself, you will always be tempted to magnify your successes while excusing your failures.

But when we see God in his holiness, we cannot help but respond with reverence and humility. And the more we experience his divine transcendence, the more we see our need for personal transformation.

Let us spend time today in awe of who God is as we enter a time of guided prayer.

GUIDED PRAYER

1. Take time to meditate on the awesomeness and majesty of God.

Imagine yourself in Isaiah's vision. See God on his throne and the seraphim around him. Hear their praise; smell the smoke; feel the shaking of the foundations of your "room." See God as he truly is.

- "There is none holy like the LORD; there is none besides you; there is no rock like our God" (1 Samuel 2:2).

2. Reflect on your own sin and shortcomings in light of his majesty and holiness.

Ask the Spirit to show you anything in your life that displeases him, then confess what comes to your thoughts with a heart of repentance.

- "Whoever conceals his transgressions will not prosper, but he who confesses and forsakes them will obtain mercy" (Proverbs 28:13).

3. Ask God to help you see yourself and others in light of his transcendent glory.

When we recognize our Lord for who he is and embrace the fact that he loves us unconditionally, we have nothing to prove to others or to ourselves.

- "When pride comes, then comes disgrace, but with the humble is wisdom" (Proverbs 11:2).

GO

The key to true humility is simple: the closer we draw to God, the further away we realize we are. In the light of his majesty, we see our fallenness. In the light of his holiness, we see our sinfulness.

But when we see our need and experience his grace, we are drawn to his transforming love. Then humility no longer becomes a goal for which we strive but the fruit of our focus on our Lord.

The same is true in our relationships with other people: the more we focus on Jesus, the less we are concerned with what they think of us or what we think of them. We no longer feel either inadequate or proud in comparison to others. And we aren't pulled away from our intimate connection with the Lord.

Pride is a temptation we all must be aware of. When you sense pride rising in your heart, turn your heart toward Jesus in prayer and praise. You will be humbled by the greatness of your God and can say like John the Baptist in John 3:30, "He must increase, but I must decrease."

As God develops in us a heart of humility, may it elevate our Savior and transform our lives, to the glory of God.

Extended reading: Psalm 95:1–7

THURSDAY

If you don't feel close to God

—

"Thus says the One who is high and lifted up, who inhabits eternity, whose name is Holy: 'I dwell in the high and holy place, and also with him who is of a contrite and lowly spirit, to revive the spirit of the lowly, and to revive the heart of the contrite.'" —Isaiah 57:15

DAY 4

My first job at a church was as a youth minister. I soon discovered that my job included doing things no other staff members wanted to do. One of them involved putting letters on the church sign each week to post whatever saying our pastor chose.

One week I posted "If you don't feel close to God, guess who moved." It's been many years, but these words stayed with me.

You and I were made for an intimate relationship with our Maker that nothing else in creation can experience. Genesis 1:26–27 lets us know that we alone are made in God's image and likeness, which enables us to connect with God as children with their father. He gave us free will so we could choose to worship him.

Most of all, his Son died for us, a fact that does not even apply to the angels, much less to the rest of creation. God does not love us because we are lovable but because "God is love," as we read in 1 John 4:8. He cannot *not* love us. He longs for personal, intimate communion with us in this life and the next.

For example, Scripture assures us in Zephaniah 3:17 that our Lord "will rejoice over you with gladness; he will quiet you by his love; he will exult over you with loud singing." The psalmist declared in Psalm 149:4, "The Lord takes pleasure in his people; he adorns the humble with salvation."

Why, then, do so many of us struggle to experience his transforming presence? Why can our worship become so formal and routine? Why does studying the Bible and praying sometimes feel like a chore? Why does the thought of worshiping God for eternity in heaven feel less than exciting?

Here's one possible answer: connecting with God requires humility.

Our Lord promises in Isaiah 57:15 that he not only dwells "in the high and holy place," but he also dwells "with him who is of a contrite and lowly spirit." When we choose a spirit of humility, he will "revive the spirit of the lowly" and "revive the heart of the contrite."

Why is humility necessary for God to move?

As we have seen this week, God can give only what we will receive. But we won't receive what we don't believe we need. If you have a new car, you're probably not shopping for another one. If you've just moved into your home, you're probably not in the housing market.

When we recognize how much we need what only God can do, we will pray for what we need and experience all that his grace desires to give.

Notes

Your attitude toward a dentist's appointment will likely be different if you are going for a routine checkup or if you have an aching tooth. After I was diagnosed with skin cancer a few years ago, my visits to the dermatologist became much more urgent.

If you're not experiencing God's transforming presence on a regular basis, ask yourself whether or not you feel like you really need him. Ask him to help you identify things in your heart and life that may be keeping him at bay and seek his help in removing any roadblocks to his presence today as we enter a time of guided prayer.

GUIDED PRAYER

1. When was the last time that worship, reading the Bible, or praying changed your life in some way?

Did you encounter God in a genuine, transforming way last Sunday in worship? In your devotional time today?

- "This is the one to whom I will look: he who is humble and contrite in spirit and trembles at my word" (Isaiah 66:2).

2. Ask the Lord for a vision of how experiencing his presence could be transforming for you.

Imagine yourself before his throne in worship. Picture him in his glory and bow before his holiness, rejoicing in his nearness and grace.

- "Oh come, let us worship and bow down; let us kneel before the LORD, our Maker!" (Psalm 95:6).

3. Tell God how much you need his presence in this moment and throughout the day.

Ask to be aware of his presence wherever you go today.

- "You will seek me and find me, when you seek me with all your heart" (Jeremiah 29:13).

GO

Choose to stay in God's holy presence as you step into your day.

Brother Lawrence noted that you can "practice the presence of God" if you follow the wisdom of 1 Thessalonians 5:16–18: "Rejoice always; pray without ceasing; give thanks in all circumstances." God is omnipresent; he isn't limited to this space. You can experience him in his heavenly glory wherever and whenever you turn your heart to him in worship and prayer today.

And would you invite others to join you? As you do, see yourself and others in the light of God's majesty. You will be empowered to love your Lord and your neighbor as your humble response of gratitude to such a gracious and powerful Father.

Extended reading: Psalm 139

FRIDAY

Surrendering superiority

—

"Do nothing from selfish ambition or conceit, but in humility count others more significant than yourselves."
—Philippians 2:3

DAY 5

Friday the 13th has an interesting story. It doesn't occur often, only once every 212 days.

The day is special to our family because my father was born on Friday, July 13, 1924. But much of our culture sees the day differently, considering today to be especially unlucky. Some say this idea actually started with the Bible: thirteen guests attended the Last Supper, including Jesus and his twelve apostles. The next day, Good Friday, Jesus was crucified.

The combination of traumatic historical events and popular culture have combined to make the day especially fearful for some. This fear even has a name: "paraskevidekatriaphobia."

About now, if you're not superstitious, you may be shrugging your intellectual shoulders in pity at those who are. It's easy to feel superior to those we consider to be wrong or less capable than we are. When someone acts irrationally, sinfully, or otherwise wrongfully, we are quick to judge and just as quick to elevate ourselves in our own minds.

I am just as vulnerable in this regard as anyone. When I meet non-Christians, I must guard against feeling superior to them for experiencing salvation that came to me only by grace, through no merits of my own, as we read in Ephesians 2. When I read or hear of sins or mistakes others make, I must guard against feeling better than they are, even though I have my own sins that they may not be committing.

This temptation reveals a problem: we cannot be looking up at God while looking down at others.

This is why our verse today is so insistent: "Do *nothing* from selfish ambition or conceit." So how do we avoid this pride in our own hearts?

Paul explains that we should "in humility count others more significant than yourselves." Notice that Paul doesn't teach us that others *are* "more significant" than we are. Instead, we are to "count" them to be so. The original Greek word here means to "consider or regard" and suggests that we are to put their well-being ahead of our own and work for their best even if it comes at personal sacrifice.

When we ask in every circumstance how we can best love God *and* our neighbor, we will position ourselves to live in humility toward both. We become humble not by seeking humility itself but through loving and serving.

And that humility will position us to experience God's power and presence in and through our lives in ways that may lead to the spiritual awakening we need so desperately today.

Notes

GUIDED PRAYER

1. Reflect on the fact that God so loved the world that he gave his Son for you (John 3:16).

Consider the generations across history that Jesus died for and express your gratitude for being a part of the family of God.

- "After this I looked, and behold, a great multitude that no one could number, from every nation, from all tribes and peoples and languages, standing before the throne and before the Lamb" (Revelation 7:9).

2. Ask the Lord to help you see people the way that he sees them.

- "Clothe yourselves, all of you, with humility toward one another" (1 Peter 5:5).

3. Pray for God to give you opportunities to love and serve someone around you today.

And ask him to give you a greater awareness of those who need to experience his love.

- "Do not use your freedom as an opportunity for the flesh, but through love serve one another" (Galatians 5:13).

GO

When we truly love someone, we will love those they love. It's not possible to fully love me if you hate my family. To put it another way, one of the best ways to love me is to love them.

When we love God with all our heart, soul, mind, and strength, this love cannot help but overflow to the people he loves all around us. One of the best ways we can demonstrate our love for God today is to love whom he loves.

John Wesley's life motto was simple but profound: "Do all the good you can by all the means you can in all the places you can at all the times you can as long as ever you can."

May God give us the grace to live by that example today.

Extended reading: John 13:1–20

SATURDAY

The best advice I've ever received

—

"He must increase, but I must decrease." —John 3:30

DAY 6

I grew up with a low self-image.

My father had a heart attack when I was two years old which severely restricted his activities as a result. He couldn't play catch with me or teach me to shoot a basketball or throw a football.

Because of that, I got picked last for all the teams during recess in elementary school. Over time, I developed a deep sense of inadequacy. It wasn't until seventh grade that I began playing tennis and discovered I actually had athletic gifts. But by then it was too late. My sense of myself was set.

I became a Christian at the age of fifteen, partially out of amazement that the God of the universe would love *me* as I am. Over the years, I've tried to base my self-esteem not on what others think of me but on who God says I am.

But it's been a challenge. I'm tempted every time I preach or with every article I write to honor God so he will honor me. I am tempted every morning to meet with God in Bible study and prayer so he will bless my day, to serve him so he will serve me. I am tempted every day to make my relationship with God a means to my ends rather than living as a means to his.

In fact, I am tempted right now to impress you with my humility in telling you about my struggles with humility.

Does any of this resonate with you?

Years ago, a wise counselor explained to me the mindset of our day: "I am not who I think I am. I am not who you think I am. I am who I think you think I am."

But there's a better way.

We can choose to live not to impress others but to humbly glorify our Lord. We can choose to say what John the Baptist said of Jesus in John 3:30: "He must increase, but I must decrease." We can imitate the One who said of himself "I am gentle and lowly in heart" (Matthew 11:29). We can follow the example of our Lord who "came not to be served but to serve, and to give his life as a ransom for many" (Mark 10:45).

The truth is that we can't live like this unless we truly believe we have nothing to prove to anyone and that we have eternal value and significance because we are eternally and unconditionally loved by our Father.

When I was in high school, my youth minister gave me the single greatest piece of advice I've ever received: *Always remember the source of your personal worth.*

To serve God with humility that seeks his glory before ours, remember the price he paid to purchase your salvation. Remember the cost of the cross. Remember that he did all of that for you and that he would do it all again, just for you.

Notes

So today, choose to serve him, not so he will love you but because he already does. Not so he will bless you, but because he already has. Love him with all your heart, soul, mind, and strength because that is how he loves you.

Always remember the source of your personal worth.

GUIDED PRAYER

1. Meditate on the death and resurrection of Jesus.

Think about how he was willing to endure immense pain and suffering for your sake, and remember what his death accomplished for you. Now imagine yourself present when he rose triumphantly from the grave. All of this he did out of joy and love for you.

- "God shows his love for us in that while we were still sinners, Christ died for us" (Romans 5:8).

2. Ask the Lord to help you experience his love for you in a tangible, personal way.

Take time to feel his presence. Receive the reality of his unconditional love.

- "The Lord your God is in your midst, a mighty one who will save; he will rejoice over you with gladness; he will quiet you by his love; he will exult over you with loud singing" (Zephaniah 3:17).

3. Think about how you can live and serve with humility as you honor the Lord in gratitude for his grace today.

- "What does the Lord require of you but to do justice, and to love kindness, and to walk humbly with your God?" (Micah 6:8).

GO

One of the best ways we can honor our Lord is by helping others honor him. As we discussed yesterday, we cannot truly love him unless we love our neighbor as well. When you choose not to live for the acclaim of others, you are free to love them whether or not they love you back. You are free to serve them whether they serve you or not.

If, like John, we are choosing to "decrease" so Jesus can "increase," we will influence others to do the same. The lighthouse that shines farthest shines brightest at home.

Extended reading: 1 John 3

SUNDAY

Reflection

DAY 7 — One of the primary themes found throughout Scripture is the importance of reflecting on what God has done so that we can internalize those lessons for when they are most needed. When Israel was wandering through the wilderness, for example, the Lord led Moses to frequently remind them of what he'd done by leading them out of Egypt (Deuteronomy 6:12) and all the ways he provided for them in the midst of their wanderings (Deuteronomy 8:2).

The purpose of that remembrance was that he knows we are forgetful creatures who, like Peter in the boat on the Sea of Galilee, are prone to pay more attention to the storms around us than the God in front of us. One of the best ways to combat that natural tendency is by creating time in your schedule dedicated to simply reflecting on what God has taught you and all that he's done for you in recent days.

To that end, we're going to take the next several Sundays in the lead-up to Holy Week as an opportunity to think back on the lessons God has taught us across the previous days. We'll spend time in prayer, asking the Lord to help us make the necessary connections to internalize those teachings to the point that they'll be there when we need them most.

My hope is that this time of focused reflection can become a pattern in your walk with the Lord that will bear fruit long after our celebration of Easter has come and gone.

We began this week by discussing how we can live a life that God can bless. From there, we examined what it means to be humble and how to see ourselves through God's eyes. Next, we talked about the importance of understanding our need for him before concluding with a look at the importance of seeing the value in both others and ourselves as a result of who we are in relationship to him.

With those lessons in mind, take a few moments now to reflect on what God has shown you. Ask him to point out anything that he particularly wants to emphasize.

When you're finished, conclude by thanking him for all he's shown you. Then ask him to use those truths to draw you closer to him and enable you to live humbly in the week to come.

Notes

WEEK THREE

Pray

MONDAY

Prayer is the gate

—

"Peter was kept in prison, but earnest prayer for him was made to God by the church." —Acts 12:5

DAY 1

Thomas Brooks was a great Puritan author and preacher who lived in the sixteenth century. In his book *Smooth Stones Taken from Ancient Brooks*, he observed that "the best and sweetest flowers of paradise God gives to his people when they are upon their knees. Prayer is the gate of heaven."

We are focusing on four necessary ingredients in a great spiritual awakening: 2 Chronicles 7:14 says that "if my people who are called by my name *humble themselves,* and *pray* and *seek my face* and *turn from their wicked ways*, then I will hear from heaven and will forgive their sin and heal their land" (emphasis added).

Last week's topic was humility; this week we will focus on prayer.

If prayer is truly "the gate of heaven," that gate has "keys" that unlock it. And over the course of this week, we'll look at seven biblical factors that enable us to pray effectively and powerfully.

We'll study one each day, beginning with the first: *pray specifically*.

Let's look at the background story to our verse for today: Herod the Great's grandson, Herod Agrippa I, was the ruler of that day. And, in an effort to gain favor with the religious authorities, he "laid violent hands on some who belonged to the church" (Acts 12:1). For example, verse 2 explains that "he killed James the brother of John with the sword." Then, not long after, he arrested Peter with the intent to have him executed after the Passover (v. 4).

But the church responded in a way that we can learn from today. Acts 12:5 tells us that "Peter was kept in prison, but earnest prayer for him was made to God by the church."

Note that "earnest," passionate prayer was offered. And it wasn't just offered by an individual, but "by the church," the entire body of Christ in collective intercession. But don't miss this fact: they prayed "for him" specifically. They prayed for Peter and his needs, asking God to deliver him from his imprisonment and pending execution.

And God answered their prayer in a dramatic way, sending an angel to free the apostle from prison. Peter then immediately went to the house where the Christians "were gathered together and were praying" (v. 12). When he knocked on the door, "a servant girl named Rhoda" was so shocked that he was there that she left him waiting outside and ran to tell the others (v .13).

I love the detail here in verse 15: "They said to her, 'You are out of your mind.' But she kept insisting that it was so." Think about it: when God answered their prayer, they didn't even believe that he had. It's so encouraging for me to know that we don't have to be perfect intercessors to pray to a perfect God. He hears us and answers us in ways that transcend us.

What impossible situation are you facing today? Who is your "Peter"?

Whoever it is, pray "for him" today. Tell God your need, as directly and intentionally as possible. Pray so specifically that you would know how to answer your prayer if you were God. Avoid generic prayers like "God be with us" (he already promised us he would be with us "always" in Matthew 28:20). Tell the Lord precisely what you are asking him to do, then trust him to answer in whatever way is best.

F. B. Meyer was right when he said, "The greatest tragedy of life is not unanswered prayer, but unoffered prayer." So offer your prayers specifically to your Father today as we enter a time of guided prayer.

GUIDED PRAYER

1. Identify a specific request you need to make to God.

- "We fasted and implored our God for this, and he listened to our entreaty" (Ezra 8:23).

2. Bring your request directly to your Father.

Tell him exactly what your need is and how you'd like him to help.

- "Casting all your anxieties on him, because he cares for you" (1 Peter 5:7).

3. If you can, write down your request in a prayer journal (or even a note on your phone), where you can record your prayers and God's answers.

Trust him to meet your needs in his perfect will and timing. Be sure to express your gratitude for his answers as they come.

- "Cast your burden on the LORD, and he will sustain you; he will never permit the righteous to be moved" (Psalm 55:22).

GO

Interceding for others is one of the greatest ways you can serve them. When we help people in our own strength, we are limited in our understanding and capabilities. When we ask God to help them, his incomprehensible knowledge and power move in response.

If you don't regularly keep a list of people you are praying for, would you begin today?

You can start by praying for your leaders as Paul encouraged Timothy to do in 1 Timothy 2:2. You can pray for your pastors and other ministers as we see in Hebrews 13:7. And you can pray "for all people" as Paul recommends in 1 Timothy 2:1. Lastly, Ephesians 6:18 reminds us to "keep alert with all perseverance, making supplication for all the saints."

As you go, give the gift of your intercession today, to the glory of God.

Extended reading: Acts 12

TUESDAY

Persistent prayer

—

"Rising very early in the morning, while it was still dark, he departed and went out to a desolate place, and there he prayed." —Mark 1:35

DAY 2

Jesus has just had a very busy day. He had taught in the synagogue at Capernaum (Mark 1:21), where he healed a man with an unclean spirit (vv. 22–28). After the service, he went to Peter's home, where he healed Peter's mother-in-law (vv. 29–31).

Then, Scripture says that "at sundown they brought to him all who were sick or oppressed by demons. And the whole city was gathered together at the door" (vv. 32–33). In response, Jesus "healed many who were sick with various diseases, and cast out many demons" (v. 34).

But now it's the next morning. Does Jesus sleep in? Does he take the day off? Hardly: Mark 1:35 says that "rising very early in the morning, while it was still dark, he departed and went out to a desolate place, and there he prayed."

This was his pattern. He prayed "early in the morning" and late at night (Matthew 14:23). One time he prayed "all night" (Luke 6:12). He prayed before meals (Matthew 14:19) and before temptation (Matthew 26:36). He prayed "by himself" (Matthew 14:23) and with crowds (Matthew 14:19). Why?

Jesus understood that prayer positions us to experience God's best. It is the means by which we connect directly with our Lord. When we read devotionals like this one, we are reading about God. When we listen to sermons, we are hearing about God. But when we pray, we are talking *to* God.

A carpenter must touch the wood he intends to shape. A surgeon must touch the body she intends to heal. When we pray, God "gets his hands on us."

This is why continual prayer is taught so consistently throughout Scripture:

- 1 Thessalonians 5:17 says, "Pray without ceasing."
- Colossians 4:2 tells us to "continue steadfastly in prayer, being watchful in it with thanksgiving."
- And Romans 12:12 calls us to "rejoice in hope, be patient in tribulation, be constant in prayer."

Jesus was clear about this as well in Matthew 7:7: "Ask, and it will be given to you; seek, and you will find; knock, and it will be opened to you." A more literal translation of the original Greek language would say, "Ask and keep on asking . . . seek and keep on seeking . . . knock and keep on knocking."

It's not that persistent prayer "wears God out," but it positions us to experience his presence and receive his grace.

So let's respond today and position ourselves before the presence and grace of God as we spend time in guided prayer.

Notes

GUIDED PRAYER

1. Meditate on Jesus' early morning prayer with his Father.

Reflect on how even Jesus, the son of God, needed to pull away from the busyness of life to pray. Think about how you can find time and space to connect with God at the beginning of each day.

- "O Lord, in the morning you hear my voice; in the morning I prepare a sacrifice for you and watch" (Psalm 5:3).

2. Reflect on Jesus' decision not only to start but also to end his days with his Father.

Think about how you can spend a few moments with God at the end of your day and share the joys and challenges you walked through. Maybe you can pick a specific time to pray with your family, or set a reminder on your phone to help point you to prayer in the evening. The important thing is to find those moments to simply stay connected.

- "When you pray, go into your room and shut the door and pray to your Father who is in secret. And your Father who sees in secret will reward you" (Matthew 6:6).

3. Ask the Holy Spirit to help you make prayer a lifestyle.

Walk through your day practicing the presence of Jesus by talking with him, listening to him, and thinking about him. Ask him to reveal his presence to you all through the day.

- "Seek the Lord and his strength; seek his presence continually!" (1 Chronicles 16:11).

GO

As we noted yesterday, one of the best ways we can serve others is by praying for them, asking our omnipotent God to meet needs we cannot meet. We can make this intercession a lifestyle, turning every problem we face into prayer. We can develop the reflex of praying at the moment the fear or challenge arises. And God will use us to bless those we know in ways we may never know on this side of eternity.

Samuel assured those he served, "Far be it from me that I should sin against the LORD by ceasing to pray for you" (1 Samuel 12:23). Who needs your prayer today?

Extended reading: Mark 1:21–45

WEDNESDAY

My favorite prayer

—

"Whatever you ask in prayer, you will receive, if you have faith." —Matthew 21:22

DAY 3

My favorite prayer in Scripture is found in an unlikely place.

In Mark 9, we find Jesus on the Mount of Transfiguration, where his heavenly glory was revealed to his closest disciples. But when they came down from the mountain, they found the other disciples arguing with a "great crowd" (v. 14).

Then a man said to Jesus, "Teacher, I brought my son to you, for he has a spirit that makes him mute. And whenever it seizes him, it throws him down, and he foams and grinds his teeth and becomes rigid. So I asked your disciples to cast it out, and they were not able" (vv. 17–18).

Jesus asked them to bring the boy to him, and verse 20 says that "when the spirit saw him, immediately it convulsed the boy, and he fell on the ground and rolled about, foaming at the mouth."

The boy's father pleaded with Jesus, "If you can do anything, have compassion on us and help us" (v. 22). And Jesus replied, "'If you can!' All things are possible for one who believes" (v. 23).

The father's response to Jesus comes next, which is my favorite prayer in the Bible. It says: "Immediately the father of the child cried out and said, 'I believe; help my unbelief!'" (v. 24). And Jesus responds to this father's vulnerable and honest prayer by healing his son (vv. 25–27).

The Bible consistently teaches us that we must pray in faith:

- "I tell you, whatever you ask in prayer, believe that you have received it, and it will be yours" (Mark 11:24).
- "Let him ask in faith, with no doubting, for the one who doubts is like a wave of the sea that is driven and tossed by the wind" (James 1:6).
- "Let us then with confidence draw near to the throne of grace, that we may receive mercy and find grace to help in time of need" (Hebrews 4:16).

But did you know that you can pray *for* faith? In fact, you can pray for the faith to have faith. You can tell God honestly, "I believe; help my unbelief!" and he will hear you and help you.

That's because faith does not *earn* God's favor—it positions us to receive his grace.

Imagine being invited to a friend's house for dinner. You must have enough faith in your friend's culinary abilities to choose to eat the food he or she prepares. Your faith didn't earn your meal, but it was essential to experiencing it.

The same is true with prayer. When you believe that God will hear you and answer you in whatever way is best, you will experience the grace he longs to give you.

And if you feel you are lacking in faith, pray for faith. Pray as this father did. You can come before God vulnerably and honestly.

Even today.

Notes

GUIDED PRAYER

1. Meditate on your Father's presence and desire to hear every prayer you offer.

- "The LORD is near to all who call on him, to all who call on him in truth" (Psalm 145:18).

2. Identify your greatest need today and trust it to him in faith.

If you are struggling to trust him, ask for the faith to have faith.

- "Call to me and I will answer you, and will tell you great and hidden things you have not known" (Jeremiah 33:3).

3. Believe that your Father has heard you and trust that he will always do what is best.

- "Do not be anxious about anything, but in everything by prayer and supplication with thanksgiving let your requests be made known to God. And the peace of God, which surpasses all understanding, will guard your hearts and your minds in Christ Jesus" (Philippians 4:6–7).

GO

George Mueller was known for his consistent life of intercession. For example, in 1844 he began praying for the conversion of five specific people. The first was converted eighteen months later, the second five years after that, and the third six years after that. Mueller prayed daily for the other two until he passed away in 1897, a total of fifty-two years. A few years after he died, both came to faith in Christ.

We don't always know how or when God will answer our prayers. But continue praying for those in need, and trust that God will hear and answer you. We may never know on this side of heaven the eternal consequences of such faithfulness.

Extended reading: Mark 11:12–24

"Whatever you ask in prayer, you will receive, if you have faith."

MATTHEW 21:22

THURSDAY

Confessing prayer

—

"If I had cherished iniquity in my heart, the Lord would not have listened." —Psalm 66:18

DAY 4

My favorite car of all time is the 1965 Ford Mustang. Mine was white with a red interior in the fastback edition with a four-on-the-floor manual transmission. It was great fun to drive and easy to maintain. And I got lots of practice at both.

One particular challenge had to do with the battery system. Cables attached to clamps that attached to posts protruding from the top of the battery. These cables, in turn, connected to the starting system, sending electricity from the battery to start the engine.

Where the clamps connected to the battery posts, corrosion was a constant problem. I actually had to keep a wire brush in the car that I could use to clean off the posts to make sure the car would start.

Otherwise, this incredible car became incredibly dead.

I share this story of my old Mustang as a parable for our souls. When we ask Jesus to become our Savior and Lord, his Spirit comes to live in us as his temple. It's his Spirit that gives us the power to be his witnesses to the entire world. And we can then speak as the Spirit leads us and pray in his power and with his guidance.

But there's a problem. Like the corrosion that blocks the power of a battery, sin blocks the power of the Holy Spirit. That's why we are told in 1 Thessalonians 5:19, "Do not quench the Spirit." It's so important for us to pray from hearts that are cleansed of sin and right with our Father. Isaiah 59:2 says, "Your iniquities have made a separation between you and your God, and your sins have hidden his face from you so that he does not hear."

The idea that God won't hear us is admittedly uncomfortable to think about, but it's important for us to unpack what today's verse teaches us. It says, "If I had cherished iniquity in my heart, the Lord would not have listened" (Psalm 66:18). It's not that God wouldn't *want* to hear us— it's that he *can't* hear us. Our sins can actually hinder and block the Holy Spirit. They drive a wedge between us and our holy Father.

In Proverbs 28:9, Solomon warned us as well: "If one turns away his ear from hearing the law, even his prayer is an abomination." But it's not all bad news! Listen to this from 1 John 1:9: "If we confess our sins, he is faithful and just to forgive us our sins and to cleanse us from all unrighteousness."

This is why the spiritual discipline of daily confession is so important. To do that, we need to ask the Lord to show us anything we must confess, then confess all he reveals. We can receive his forgiving grace and continue forward without guilt or shame. His forgiveness and acceptance are immediate and complete. And, as a result, he is able to hear all our prayers and answer according to his will.

Notes

Peter assured us in 1 Peter 3:12, "The eyes of the Lord are on the righteous, and his ears are open to their prayer. But the face of the Lord is against those who do evil."

Let us be people who practice daily confession and experience the open ears of God. May we be willing to come before God today with a repentant heart as we spend time in guided prayer.

GUIDED PRAYER

1. Ask the Lord to bring to mind anything you need to confess.

Feel free to write down what comes to your thoughts in a private journal or note. Be specific and honest.

- "Whoever conceals his transgressions will not prosper, but he who confesses and forsakes them will obtain mercy" (Proverbs 28:13).

2. Now admit each of your sins specifically to your Father.

Receive his promise to forgive you and to cleanse your mind and heart today. If you wrote them down, throw away the paper or delete the note and celebrate the grace of God you've received.

- "I acknowledged my sin to you, and I did not cover my iniquity; I said, 'I will confess my transgressions to the Lord,' and you forgave the iniquity of my sin" (Psalm 32:5).

3. Go to your Father in prayer, confident that you are heard and welcomed.

He is eager to share his love and presence with you right now.

- "We do not have a high priest who is unable to sympathize with our weaknesses, but one who in every respect has been tempted as we are, yet without sin. Let us then with confidence draw near to the throne of grace, that we may receive mercy and find grace to help in time of need" (Hebrews 4:15–16).

GO

Dwight Moody said that he sought to "keep short accounts" with God. He ended every day by reviewing his day with the Lord and confessing anything the Spirit brought to mind. That way, he could sleep peacefully and rise to meet God in the morning with confidence.

"Short accounts" are essential not just for our souls but also for our intercession. 1 Peter 4:7 says that we are to "be self-controlled and sober-minded for the sake of your prayers." This is also true for the sake of those we pray for.

Charles Spurgeon shared, "No man can do me a truer kindness in this world than to pray for me." Whom will you be kind to today?

Extended reading: Psalm 51

FRIDAY

Knocking on God's door at midnight

—

"If you then, who are evil, know how to give good gifts to your children, how much more will the heavenly Father give the Holy Spirit to those who ask him!" —Luke 11:13

DAY 5

In Luke 6:5–9, Jesus told a story about a man who knocked on his neighbor's door at midnight and said, "Friend, lend me three loaves, for a friend of mine has arrived on a journey, and I have nothing to set before him." The man inside the house replied, "Do not bother me; the door is now shut, and my children are with me in bed. I cannot get up and give you anything."

However, Jesus continued, "I tell you, though he will not get up and give him anything because he is his friend, yet because of his impudence he will rise and give him whatever he needs." Jesus followed this story by telling us to ask, seek, and knock, with the promise that God will answer us.

He illustrated: If your son asks for a fish, would you give him a serpent? If he asked for an egg, would you give him a scorpion? He concluded: "If you then, who are evil, know how to give good gifts to your children, how much more will the heavenly Father give the Holy Spirit to those who ask him!"

Jesus' meaning seems clear: if we pray long enough and passionately enough, God will give us what we ask because of our "impudence" (the original Greek word here means "shamelessness" or "lack of proper restraint"). It seems like the implication is that God doesn't want to answer. Remember, the man inside the house said, "Do not bother me; the door is now shut." The story seems to suggest that if we bother him long enough and loudly enough, he will answer our prayers.

In fact, the story teaches just the opposite.

Typical homes in Jesus' culture had only one room. The front two-thirds was a dirt floor where the animals were kept at night; the back one-third was an elevated platform where the family slept together. The door was open all day since hospitality was an important value and there was little to steal. It was only "shut" when the family went to sleep.

In a day without preservatives, people made bread each day for that day's needs (hence Jesus' reference to "our daily bread" in the Model Prayer). But this neighbor in the parable didn't do so. Then, when he needed bread for a visitor, he banged on a door that was shut, waking the family and animals inside. The man didn't want to get up to help, but the neighbor's persistence forced his hand until he did.

Here's the key: Jesus is using a rabbinic teaching technique known as the *qal wahomer*, meaning "from the light to the heavy." His point is that if a man would get up at midnight to give his neighbor bread, *how much more* would God rise to answer our prayers and meet our needs.

Because of that, when we pray, we should *expect* our Father to hear us and give us what is best. Not because we are worthy of his grace but because "God is love," as the Scriptures tell us in 1 John 4:8. He *always* and *only* wants what is best for his children. His will is *always* "good and acceptable and perfect," as we read in Romans 12:2.

We should not assume that we know the best answer to our prayers. But we should expect that our Father does and trust him to do what results in his greatest glory and our greatest good.

GUIDED PRAYER

1. Meditate on Jesus' story.

Imagine yourself inside the house as the neighbor bangs on your door. Feel the man's frustration, then contrast his anger with our Father's grace.

- "From his fullness we have all received, grace upon grace" (John 1:16).

2. Remember the last prayer your Father answered.

Was it a sin he forgave? A need he met? A blessing he gave? Reflect on the grace in which he heard you and answered you.

- "Before they call I will answer; while they are yet speaking I will hear" (Isaiah 65:24).

3. Name your greatest need today and bring it to your Father by faith.

Continue to pray until he answers with his best. Remember his Son's sacrifice for you and trust his transforming love.

- "The Word became flesh and dwelt among us, and we have seen his glory, glory as of the only Son from the Father, full of grace and truth" (John 1:14).

GO

Alfred Lord Tennyson wrote, "More things are wrought by prayer than this world dreams of." Paul would have agreed. He not only prayed for his readers; he regularly asked them to pray for him as well (cf. Colossians 4:3; Philippians 1:19; 2 Thessalonians 3:1–5; Romans 15:30–32; 2 Corinthians 1:11; 1 Thessalonians 5:25).

Who is praying regularly for you? For whom are you interceding regularly? James warned us, "You do not have, because you do not ask."

Expect your Father to hear you and to answer you. Then give the gift of intercession to someone who needs it most today.

Extended reading: Luke 18:1–8

SATURDAY

Drawing on God's bank account

—

"Whatever you ask in my name, this I will do, that the Father may be glorified in the Son. If you ask me anything in my name, I will do it." —John 14:13–14

DAY 6

One of my early childhood memories is of going to the grocery store with my mother. After she loaded our cart with food, she pushed it (with me inside) to the checkout counter. There the cashier rang up our purchases and told my mother the total. Mom then took out a piece of paper from her purse, filled in the amount, signed her name, and handed it to the cashier.

This seemed like magic to me.

I couldn't understand what made this small piece of paper so valuable. Years later, I learned about bank accounts and checkbooks and discovered this simple fact: a check is only as good as the funds on which it is drawn.

Mom could sign her name to a million-dollar check, but that wouldn't make her check worth a million dollars.

However, if a billionaire signed his name to a check, that would be a different story.

This is the principle behind Jesus' amazing promise in our verse today: "Whatever you ask in my name, this I will do, that the Father may be glorified in the Son. If you ask me anything in my name, I will do it."

To pray in Jesus' "name" means to "draw on his account," to depend on his omnipotence. It means that we are asking him to answer us not because of our merit but out of his grace.

This humility is important to correct a frequent misunderstanding about prayer.

In our post-Christian culture, it's easy to get the idea that basic Christian activities like prayer are an accomplishment and worthy of a divine response. If we get up early to pray, even better. If we pray consistently, our faith must have reached another spiritual tier. It's as though we deserve for our prayers to be answered simply because we prayed them.

The opposite is actually true.

We have no achievements that we can draw on, no "money" in our bank to withdraw. Anything God does in answer to our prayers is the result of his grace, not our accomplishments.

So when we pray "in Jesus' name," this means far more than simply adding these words to the end of our prayer. It means that we acknowledge we have nothing to offer but are appealing to the grace of God and his generous sacrifice and love.

We "sign Jesus' name" to our check so it is drawn on his "account."

Notes

GUIDED PRAYER

1. Meditate on your Father's omnipotence.

Reflect on the power that spoke the universe into being.

- "Great is our Lord, and abundant in power; his understanding is beyond measure" (Psalm 147:5).

2. Reflect on how little you have to offer in light of God's greatness.

- "Woe is me! For I am lost; for I am a man of unclean lips, and I dwell in the midst of a people of unclean lips; for my eyes have seen the King, the Lord of hosts!" (Isaiah 6:5).

3. Bring your needs to your Father with humble dependence on his grace.

- "God is able to make all grace abound to you, so that having all sufficiency in all things at all times, you may abound in every good work" (2 Corinthians 9:8).

GO

Your needs are greater than you can meet, or you wouldn't need to pray about them. The same is true for those who need your intercession today. God offers us good news in 2 Corinthians 12:9 when he says, "My grace is sufficient for you, for my power is made perfect in weakness."

When we pray for a great spiritual awakening to sweep our land, when we intercede for friends and family facing overwhelming odds, when we ask God to do what only God can do, we are positioning ourselves properly before our omnipotent Father. So let's continue to pray in expectant humility. The greater your needs, the greater the opportunity to reveal his power and demonstrate his grace.

Will you ask God to reveal his power and grace in answer to your prayers today?

Extended reading: Revelation 19:1–16

"Whatever you ask in my name, this I will do, that the Father may be glorified in the Son. If you ask me anything in my name, I will do it."

JOHN 14:13-14

SUNDAY

Reflection

DAY 7

As we conclude this week's focus on prayer, spend today reflecting on what the Lord has taught you. We began by learning how to pray specifically and persistently before continuing with a look at what it means to pray in faith. From there, we examined what it means to pray confessionally, expectantly, and humbly, with the latter tying back into last week's focus on walking humbly with God.

When you think back on those aspects of prayer, are there any that stand out as particular areas where you struggle? Are there any that seem to come more naturally to you? And are there where you feel the Lord challenging you to improve?

As you reflect on these questions, be sure to include the Lord in the conversation. After all, at its heart prayer is a conversation between you and God. As such, trying to understand the way in which we should pray should be a conversation with him as well.

"Let us then with confidence draw near to the throne of grace, that we may receive mercy and find grace to help in time of need."

HEBREWS 4:16

WEEK FOUR

Seek

MONDAY

You were made for a purpose

—

"O God, you are my God; earnestly I seek you; my soul thirsts for you; my flesh faints for you, as in a dry and weary land where there is no water." —Psalm 63:1

DAY 1

I love putting together puzzles. I've never been extremely fast at them, but still it's one of my favorite ways to spend time with friends and family. One critical rule of jigsaw puzzles that makes the entire experience work is this: a piece is made for only one place in the puzzle. It's what makes assembling a puzzle so rewarding.

The same is true of our souls. We were made for one specific purpose: intimacy with our Maker. God created us in his image and likeness so we could experience a personal relationship with him that nothing else in creation can know. From the first moments in the Garden of Eden to today, he longs for the kind of intimacy that fathers have with their children (1 John 3:1) and husbands with their wives (Ephesians 5:25–32).

This truth led to a phrase commonly attributed to Blaise Pascal in his collection of writing fragments called the *Pensées*. He said there is a God-shaped emptiness in each of us. Pascal's full observation was actually even more profound. And even more relevant to our souls today.

Pascal was born in 1623 and was a true genius. He wrote an essay on geometry at the age of seventeen that managed to make even René Descartes jealous. Two years later, he developed the first digital calculator. He also invented the syringe, created the hydraulic press, and laid the foundation for the modern theory of probabilities.

But his understanding of human experience was just as brilliant as his scientific expertise. For instance, he observed that "all men seek happiness. There are no exceptions. However different the means they may employ, they all strive towards this goal. The reason why some go to war and some do not is the same desire in both, but interpreted in two different ways. The will never takes the least step except to that end."

He also asked, "What else does this craving, and this helplessness, proclaim but that there was once in man a true happiness, of which all that now remains is the empty print and trace?"

His answer to this question was profound: "This he tries in vain to fill with everything around him, seeking in things that are not there the help he cannot find in those that are, though none can help, since this infinite abyss can be filled only with an infinite and immutable object; in other words, by God himself."

Pascal concluded: "God alone is man's true good, and since man abandoned him, it is a strange fact that nothing in nature has been found to take his place."

David agreed when he prayed: "O God, you are my God; earnestly I seek you; my soul thirsts for you; my flesh faints for you, as in a dry and weary land where there is no water" (Psalm 63:1).

Notes

If your soul is feeling thirsty and faint today, maybe the very thing you need is time in the presence of God. Connect with him today as we spend time in guided prayer.

GUIDED PRAYER

1. Reflect on the fact that you were made for intimacy with your Maker.

- "He made from one man every nation of mankind to live on all the face of the earth, having determined allotted periods and the boundaries of their dwelling place, that they should seek God, and perhaps feel their way toward him and find him. Yet he is actually not far from each one of us" (Acts 17:26–27).

2. Would you say you are experiencing personal intimacy with God?

Would he agree? If not, ask the Holy Spirit to show you anything blocking your relationship with your Father, confess what comes to your thoughts, and step back into intimacy with your Lord.

- "Whoever conceals his transgressions will not prosper, but he who confesses and forsakes them will obtain mercy" (Proverbs 28:13).

3. Ask the Spirit to help you choose intimacy with your Lord as your first priority each day.

Settle for nothing less than a transformative personal relationship with your Father.

- "You have said, 'Seek my face.' My heart says to you, 'Your face, Lord, do I seek'" (Psalm 27:8).

GO

Knowing God intimately is the purpose you were made for, a fact that is just as true for the people you know as it is for you.

How can you extend God's invitation to intimacy with those around you today? Set an example with a life filled with passion for your Lord. Then ask the Spirit to use you as a catalyst for such renewal in the lives you influence.

Spiritual awakenings begin with personal awakenings. May that be true of us and those we know, to the glory of God.

Extended reading: Psalm 63

TUESDAY

With all your heart

—

"You will seek me and find me, when you seek me with all your heart." —Jeremiah 29:13

DAY 2

Have you ever experienced God in a sunrise? Have you sensed his presence during a walk on the beach or a hike through the woods?

Most of us have times when we sense God's nearness. At other times, he feels far from us. I can offer personal examples: navigating the stress of rush-hour traffic when I'm late to a meeting I'd rather not attend. Or sitting with someone going through intense grief I'm not able to lessen. Or watching news reports of tragedies I cannot prevent.

It certainly seems that there are "God moments" and there are "rest of life moments." But this is not the way God created it to be. He wants to be as close to us in the hard times as in the good times. He promises us in Isaiah 43:2 that "when you pass through the waters, I will be with you." John 11:35 tells us that he grieves as we grieve and feels every pain we feel.

God wants us to experience the power and strength of his presence in every moment of every day.

As we noted in yesterday's devotional, we have been conditioned to seek God on Sunday and during religious activities but not during the rest of the week. We tend to turn to God in the good times and turn from him in the bad times.

But if you can learn to seek him "with all your heart," every moment of every day, in every circumstance of life, he promises, "You will seek me and find me." He longs for this kind of constant intimacy with you. Our Father wants his children to experience his best constantly and consistently.

To do that, we may need to develop the reflex of seeking God in every moment of the day. Ask him to reveal himself in your circumstances and in other people. Ask him to make his presence real to you in the experiences of your day. Look for him at work as you work; listen for his voice in your soul. Read and memorize Scripture, then recall its words as they apply to the decisions and challenges of your day.

In *The Pursuit of God*, A. W. Tozer noted, "The facts are that God is not silent, has never been silent. It is the nature of God to speak. The second person of the Trinity is called the Word. The Bible is the inevitable outcome of God's continuous speech. It is the infallible declaration of his mind for us put into our familiar human words."

Would God say you are seeking him today with your "whole heart"?

Notes

GUIDED PRAYER

1. Reflect on God's desire to speak in every dimension and circumstance of your life.

- "My sheep hear my voice, and I know them, and they follow me" (John 10:27).

2. Take time to experience God's presence in his creation.

Step outside if you can to meet him in nature. If you cannot do this, focus on images or memories of nature. Think about the attributes of your Creator on display in his creation.

- "The heavens declare the glory of God, and the sky above proclaims his handiwork. Day to day pours out speech, and night to night reveals knowledge. There is no speech, nor are there words, whose voice is not heard" (Psalm 19:1–3).

3. Now ask the Spirit to help you seek God with your "whole" heart throughout your day, looking for his presence and sensing his grace.

- "You will seek the LORD your God and you will find him, if you search after him with all your heart and with all your soul" (Deuteronomy 4:29).

Notes

GO

Seeking God holistically is a choice we can make. In fact, it is a choice we are commanded to make: 1 Chronicles 22:19 says, "Set your mind and heart to seek the LORD your God."

This is also a choice we can model and offer to others. If they see the transforming difference the presence of God makes in our lives, they will be drawn to him and the peace we experience.

Leonard Ravenhill asked, "If you have the smile of God, what does it matter if you have the frown of men?" Share the smile of God with those who need what you have and you will spark spiritual awakening one person at a time.

Extended reading: Psalm 119:1–8

WEDNESDAY

God is not a hobby

—

"Seek first the kingdom of God and his righteousness, and all these things will be added to you." —Matthew 6:33

DAY 3

Have you ever had the chance to visit a castle? Maybe it was a castle still being used today, like in Great Britain. Or maybe it was a medieval structure left over from long ago.

For those of us who live in a democracy, buildings like this and the royalty they represent can feel strange to us. Americans even fought a war for independence to be freed from the rule of kings. And one of the nation's core beliefs is that we as people can and should govern ourselves.

But Jesus began his earthly ministry in a very different way than we might expect in our culture. He said in Mark 1:15, "The time is fulfilled, and the kingdom of God is at hand; repent and believe in the gospel." He taught us to "seek first the kingdom of God and his righteousness" in Matthew 6:33. He instructed us to pray, "Your kingdom come, your will be done, on earth as it is in heaven" in Matthew 6:10. And in Revelation 19:16 we read that when Jesus returns, his name will be "King of kings and Lord of lords."

The Bible describes God as "the King of the ages, immortal, invisible" (1 Timothy 1:17). Scripture proclaims, "The Lord is the true God; he is the living God and the everlasting King" (Jeremiah 10:10).

So when the Bible describes God as king, it is referring to God as king of every dimension of the universe, every moment of every day. Everything we think we own actually comes from him and is to be used for his purposes. In a very real sense, you are wearing your king's clothes right now, breathing his air, walking on his planet.

And he is the king of Monday, not just Sunday. He is the king of what you do in private, not just what you do in public. He is the king of the money you keep, not just the money you give. He is the king of every part of your life, every day of your life.

Tragically, many in our culture treat God not as a king but as a hobby. They see him as relevant to their religious activities but not the rest of their lives. Some might play golf on Sunday, I might go to church, and someone else might go to a museum—they are all hobbies, ways we spend our free time.

Of course, no one has the right to force their hobbies on others. I can't make you like classical music any more than you can make me like opera. In the same way, I have no right to force my religious hobby on you. Or so our secularized culture thinks. In the same way, why would we expect others to care about our religious "hobby" if it's nothing more than a choice on how we spend our Sunday mornings?

Here's the problem: when we make God anything less than our king, we miss out on all he has planned for and through our lives. We miss his perfect will, his providential

Notes

purpose, and his abiding presence. We miss all the ways he will make our lives significant in this life and the next. We are left with what we as finite, fallen humans can do. And that's not nearly what he can do.

Would you make God your king today?

Let's seek his kingdom first by doing his will in every moment of our days. Jesus' promise is clear in our verse today: "Seek first the kingdom of God and his righteousness, and all these things will be added to you."

Choose to seek his kingdom first today by opening your heart and mind to the king in guided prayer.

GUIDED PRAYER

1. Reflect on God's role as the king of the universe.

- "I saw the Lord sitting upon a throne, high and lifted up; and the train of his robe filled the temple" (Isaiah 6:1).

2. Ask his Spirit to reveal any areas of your life that are not submitted to his kingship, then choose to make him king of your entire life.

- "Humble yourselves, therefore, under the mighty hand of God so that at the proper time he may exalt you" (1 Peter 5:6).

3. Seek to advance God's kingdom by doing his will in every area of your life.

- "Proclaiming the kingdom of God and teaching about the Lord Jesus Christ with all boldness and without hindrance" (Acts 28:31).

GO

We can't expect the world to treat our Lord any better than we treat him. If Jesus is our religious hobby rather than our holistic king, others will view him in the same way. But if we submit every dimension of our lives to his lordship, others will see the difference his Spirit makes in a life that is fully his.

A. W. Tozer observed, "If we cooperate with him in loving obedience, God will manifest himself to us, and that manifestation will be the difference between a nominal Christian life and a life radiant with the light of his face."

Extended reading: Revelation 7

THURSDAY

Praying like Abraham Lincoln

—

"Call to me and I will answer you, and will tell you great and hidden things that you have not known." —Jeremiah 33:3

DAY 4

My father-in-law was amazing. He built his own house, doing much of the work himself. He could repair anything on a car or a truck. He was a hunter and a fisherman. After taking early retirement from his business career, he led a volunteer fire station, designed an in-home ministry for senior adults in his community, and ran a full-time farm with my mother-in-law.

I, on the other hand, can do none of the things I just described (except catch fish on occasion). The good news is, I know people like my father-in-law. And if I am humble enough to admit what I don't know and ask for help when I need it (which is often), everything works out.

If only I were always this wise with God.

Three months after Abraham Lincoln was assassinated, a writer named Noah Brooks reported that the great president once said, "I have been driven many times upon my knees by the overwhelming conviction that I had nowhere else to go. My own wisdom and that of all about me seemed insufficient for that day."

And just as God was willing and able to hear the prayers of President Lincoln, he is ready to answer our prayers today. In fact, he assures us, "Call to me and I will answer you, and will tell you great and hidden things that you have not known" (Jeremiah 33:3).

But we must "call" to him. Isaiah 55:6 says that we must "seek the LORD while he may be found" and "call upon him while he is near." And we must decide that "as for me, I would seek God, and to God would I commit my cause" (Job 5:8).

When we do, he is ready to hear us and to help us. But there's a catch: we must seek him for his glory, not ours. Our desire should be to know him for the sake of knowing him as our Father and king. When we seek him primarily for what he can do for us, we are not seeking God but only his blessings.

Meister Eckhart was right: "If we seek God for our own good and profit, we are not seeking God." And, in *My Utmost for His Highest,* Oswald Chambers warned us: "Spiritual lust causes me to demand an answer from God, instead of seeking God himself who gives the answer."

Seek God himself today as we enter a time of guided prayer.

Notes

GUIDED PRAYER

1. Reflect on your Father's desire to bless his children.

- "Fear not, little flock, for it is your Father's good pleasure to give you the kingdom" (Luke 12:32).

2. Name your greatest need for divine wisdom or help and trust it to your Lord.

- "Whatever you ask in prayer, believe that you have received it, and it will be yours" (Mark 11:24).

3. Ask the Spirit to help you seek God for the sake of knowing God.

- "The LORD looks down from heaven on the children of man, to see if there are any who understand, who seek after God" (Psalm 14:2).

GO

Again from *My Utmost for His Highest*, Oswald Chambers observed, "Prayer is the way that the life of God in us is nourished. . . . We look upon prayer simply as a means of getting things for ourselves, but the biblical purpose of prayer is that we may get to know God himself."

One way to seek to do that is to seek him in community. When we pray in agreement, our prayers are powerful (Matthew 18:19). When we worship together, we join heaven's community of praise (cf. Revelation 7:9–10). When we seek God with our fellow believers for no reason except to know God, we experience him in ways that transform our faith and empower our witness (cf. Acts 1:8; 2:1–4).

Whom will you seek God with today?

Extended reading: Colossians 3:1–17

"Call to me and I will answer you, and will tell you great and hidden things that you have not known."

JEREMIAH 33:3

FRIDAY

A door with no handle

—

"Behold, I stand at the door and knock. If anyone hears my voice and opens the door, I will come in to him and eat with him, and he with me." —Revelation 3:20

DAY 5

In the Keble College chapel on the campus of Oxford University is a painting created by the famous artist Holman Hunt.

The masterpiece is titled "The Light of the World." It brings to life Jesus' declaration to the church at Laodicea in Revelations 3:20, "Behold, I stand at the door and knock. If anyone hears my voice and opens the door, I will come in to him and eat with him, and he with me."

As Hunt depicts the scene, Jesus stands at a door, lantern in hand. Vines are growing on the ground with unclaimed fruit at Jesus' feet. The painting is stunning in its precision.

However, it is missing one detail: the door has no handle on Jesus' side.

The reason is simple: the handle of our heart is on our side of the door. Jesus must stand at the door and knock. Only when we choose to open the door can we experience the fullness of his presence.

The good news is, when we open the door, God promises that he "will" come in and eat with us. It's not that he simply "could" or he "might," but Jesus wants us to have an intimate, transforming, daily relationship with him. He *wants* us to experience the joy of fellowship with our Savior.

In fact, he is knocking at the door of your heart right now.

Scripture promises us in James 4:8: "Draw near to God, and he will draw near to you." And David, the psalmist, said of our Lord, "Those who know your name put their trust in you, for you, O Lord, have not forsaken those who seek you" (Psalm 9:10).

Scripture assures us that "The Lord is good to those who wait for him, to the soul who seeks him" (Lamentations 3:25). And we are told in Psalms, "The young lions suffer want and hunger; but those who seek the Lord lack no good thing" (Psalm 34:10).

Jesus' promise is clear: "Ask, and it will be given to you; seek, and you will find; knock, and it will be opened to you. For everyone who asks receives, and the one who seeks finds, and to the one who knocks it will be opened" (Matthew 7:7–8). We are not waiting on God—he is waiting on us.

A small girl and her father once stood before Hunt's painting at Keble College. They admired it for many minutes. Then the girl turned to her father and asked, "Daddy, did he ever get in?"

God is standing at the door of your heart today. Let him in as we spend time in guided prayer.

Notes

GUIDED PRAYER

1. Reflect on your Savior's desire for fellowship with you.

- "The thief comes only to steal and kill and destroy. I came that they may have life and have it abundantly" (John 10:10).

2. Take time to experience his presence.

Intentionally open the "door" of your heart to him. Welcome him into your life so you can have an intimate relationship with your heavenly Father.

- "Before they call I will answer; while they are yet speaking I will hear" (Isaiah 65:24).

3. Choose to make intimacy with Jesus a lifestyle.

Think about how you can invite him into your life throughout your day. Where can you find small moments to reconnect with him in the midst of today's activities?

- "May all who seek you rejoice and be glad in you! May those who love your salvation say evermore, 'God is great!'" (Psalm 70:4).

Notes

GO

In a sermon, Charles Spurgeon observed, "The sacred promises, though in themselves most sure and precious, are of no avail for the comfort and sustenance of the soul unless you grasp them by faith, plead them in prayer, expect them by hope, and receive them with gratitude."

Of all God's promises, the promise of his presence is foundational to the rest. So, when you open the door of your heart to your Savior, invite others to join you. Make time to experience him together in community and in worship. He will speak to you through your fellow believers and to them through you.

As the "body of Christ" (1 Corinthians 12:27), you will experience more fully the fullness of Christ. And you will answer Jesus' prayer that his followers "may all be one" (John 17:21), to the glory of God the Father.

Extended reading: Ephesians 4

SATURDAY

Entering a sterile room

—

"The Lord is righteous; he loves righteous deeds; the upright shall behold his face." —Psalm 11:7

DAY 6

I remember vividly the first time I visited a person in the hospital who had just undergone surgery. Signs were posted outside his room forbidding entry to anyone who was not fully prepared. Nurses helped me into surgical clothing; I had to put a cap on my head and a mask on my face. I had to wash my hands thoroughly with antiseptic foam. Only then could I step into the room.

The reason was simple: because of his condition, his body had not yet regained its natural immunities. A single germ introduced into this sterile environment could kill the person I came to encourage. Every precaution was essential to safeguarding his life.

In a similar fashion, our holy God lives in a perfect heaven. Even a single sin would corrupt his paradise. This is why

Jesus had to die to pay the debt for our sins so they could be not only forgiven but also removed from us "as far as the east is from the west" (Psalm 103:12).

What is true in heaven is also true on earth. Confessing our sins and being forgiven and cleansed from them is essential to intimacy with our Father. He promises us, "Whoever conceals his transgressions will not prosper, but he who confesses and forsakes them will obtain mercy" (Proverbs 28:13). But we must confess and forsake them to receive the grace he longs to give us.

This principle is central to our week's emphasis on seeking God's face. In Zephaniah 2:3, the prophet Zephaniah called God's people to "seek the Lord, all you humble of the land, who do his just commands; seek righteousness; seek humility." And in Psalm 11:7, David observed, "The Lord is righteous; he loves righteous deeds; the upright shall behold his face."

This is not legalism or works-based righteousness. It is not that we must earn God's favor or presence. Rather, this is our response to God's great grace: when we confess our sins to him, he cleanses us and calls us into his throne room in love.

Hosea 10:12 is God's call to us today: "Sow for yourselves righteousness; reap steadfast love; break up your fallow ground, for it is time to seek the Lord, that he may come and rain righteousness upon you."

Hear that again: "It is time to seek the Lord."

So let's do that together as we enter a time of guided prayer.

Notes

GUIDED PRAYER

1. Reflect on your Father's desire to share his presence with you.

- "The Word became flesh and dwelt among us, and we have seen his glory, glory as of the only Son from the Father, full of grace and truth" (John 1:14).

2. Ask the Spirit to show you anything that would hinder your worship, then confess what comes to your thoughts and claim your Father's forgiveness.

- "Repent therefore, and turn back, that your sins may be blotted out" (Acts 3:19).

3. Pray for the strength to refuse temptation and to choose holiness that you can continue to walk in intimacy with your Lord.

- "God has not called us for impurity, but in holiness" (1 Thessalonians 4:7).

GO

Living in holiness is both a vertical and horizontal practice. To experience the presence of our holy God, we must be holy with him and with each other. We cannot love our Lord with all our heart, soul, mind, and strength unless we also love our neighbor as ourselves (Mark 12:30–31).

This is why Scripture urges us, "Strive for peace with everyone, and for the holiness without which no one will see the Lord" (Hebrews 12:14).

Extended reading: 1 Peter 1

"The Lord is righteous; he loves righteous deeds; the upright shall behold his face."

PSALM 11:7

SUNDAY

Reflection

DAY 7

This week we've discussed what it means to seek God's face. It's a concept that sounds like it should come naturally to those who are in a personal relationship with the Lord, but the ethereal nature of communing with our heavenly Father can make it difficult on a practical level.

As such, we started our conversation by discussing how God made us for intimacy with him before moving on to see how that intimacy requires our full devotion. We talked about how we must seek God's kingdom above everything and everyone else while also discussing the need to do so for his glory rather than our own.

From there, we moved on to examine God's promise that when we seek his face in the manner described above, we will find him. Finally, we concluded with a discussion on how confession and the desire to be holy should flow naturally from an encounter with our most holy God.

As you reflect on those truths, ask the Lord to help you know if there are any ways in which you have not sought his face in the manner prescribed by his word. Do you seek his face out of a genuine desire for a relationship with him or from a sense of obligation and the knowledge that you should want such a relationship? If it's the latter, know that God's response is not judgment for the ways in which you might fall short but the desire to help you move beyond them to encounter him in new and authentic ways.

Will you let him?

"You will seek me
and find me, when
you seek me with all
your heart."

JEREMIAH 29:13

WEEK FIVE

Turn

MONDAY

I am directionally challenged

—

"God, be merciful to me, a sinner!"
—Luke 18:13

DAY 1

I am what my wife calls "directionally challenged." When we are driving, I never know north from south from east from west. I can drive to a location ten times and get lost going there on the eleventh trip. Part of my problem is that I often *think* I am right when I am in fact wrong.

And, like most people, I am reluctant to change my course if I think my course is correct.

What is true for my driving is true for our souls: if we do not think our ways are "wicked," we are unlikely to "turn" from them. And in our culture today, the word *wicked* itself seems to be antiquated, or simply no longer relevant as the world normalizes moral relativism.

But let's consider this parable in Luke today.

Jesus told a story about two men who went up to the temple in Jerusalem to pray, one a Pharisee and the other a tax collector. The Pharisee, "standing by himself, prayed thus: 'God, I thank you that I am not like other men, extortioners, unjust adulterers, or even like this tax collector. I fast twice a week; I give tithes of all that I get'" (Luke 18:11–12).

Jesus is not exaggerating—this is how Pharisees saw themselves. They were the spiritual elite of their day. Never more than six thousand in number, they were considered to be the holiest men in Israel. They fasted twice a week, even though the Law required only one fast a year, on the Day of Atonement, and they tithed on everything they received, not just their crops, as instructed in Deuteronomy 14:22–27.

By contrast, "the tax collector, standing far off, would not even lift up his eyes to heaven, but beat his breast, saying, 'God, be merciful to me, a sinner!'" (Luke 18:13–14). Those who listened to Jesus' story would be nodding their heads in agreement since tax collectors were the most despised people in their culture.

When Rome conquered a nation, they usually hired locals to collect taxes on their behalf. This person could take as much as he liked, with Roman protection, so long as he gave the Empire what it asked. No wonder the man says in the Greek, "God be merciful to me *the* sinner!"

Now comes the shock: Jesus said, "I tell you, this man," the tax collector, "went down to his house justified, rather than the other. For everyone who exalts himself will be humbled, but the one who humbles himself will be exalted" (v. 14).

What Jesus is telling us is that if we think our ways aren't "wicked" and sinful, then we're a lot like the Pharisee who was oblivious to his own faults. Yet if we agree that we must "turn" from our ways with humility and repentance, we're like the tax collector who walks in humility. And it's only that path of humility that allows us to change course toward true spiritual awakening.

Let us choose wisely today.

Notes

GUIDED PRAYER

1. Reflect on the fact that, no matter how your culture sees you or you see yourself, you are a sinner.

- "If we say we have no sin, we deceive ourselves, and the truth is not in us" (1 John 1:8).

2. Consider the fact that your sins cost Jesus the cross.

- "Christ also suffered once for sins, the righteous for the unrighteous, that he might bring us to God, being put to death in the flesh but made alive in the Spirit" (1 Peter 3:18).

3. Ask the Spirit to help you see your sins as God sees them, then repent and claim his forgiving grace.

- "If we confess our sins, he is faithful and just to forgive us our sins and to cleanse us from all unrighteousness" (1 John 1:9).

GO

Rick Warren observed, "When you've experienced grace and you feel like you've been forgiven, you're a lot more forgiving of other people. You're a lot more gracious to others."

Have you "turned" from your "wicked ways" today? Have you experienced God's forgiving love? If so, are there others in your life who need this gift today? Who needs your forgiveness just as you need God's?

Let's pay forward the grace of God today.

Extended reading: Psalm 103

*"God, be merciful to
me, a sinner!"*

—LUKE 18:13

TUESDAY

Jesus' most surprising apostle

—

"As Jesus passed on from there, he saw a man named Matthew sitting at the tax booth, and he said to him, 'Follow me.' And he rose and followed him." —Matthew 9:9

DAY 2

Being a tax collector was the most despised and immoral job in the Roman Empire. As we noted yesterday, tax collectors gathered revenue for the hated Romans and could collect all they wanted so long as they gave the Empire its share. But there's more to the story.

Cicero, a Roman politician and writer, declared tax collectors and lenders to be the two worst trades.

And yet the Jews despised tax collectors even more than the rest of their ancient society. Tax collectors could not testify in court as a witness, for they were assumed to be liars. They could not even attend worship in the temple or synagogue, for they were considered unclean.

The reason for such disgust with tax collectors was simple: these men were cheating traitors. Rome hired them to tax their own friends and neighbors, collecting money on behalf of the enemy. And because they could tax as much as they wanted, they became thieves, taking well beyond what they needed in order to line their own increasingly wealthy pockets.

They taxed their fellow Jews on their grain, wine, fruit, and oil. They taxed their income and their commerce. They taxed those who crossed a bridge or used a road or a harbor. They could stop anyone, anywhere, examine his goods, and assess whatever taxes he wished. If the man could not pay what the tax collector required, he could loan him the money at an impossible rate of interest.

Matthew was one such tax collector. He did his work in Capernaum, where he taxed travelers along the great road to Damascus which came through their town. He taxed those who worked on the Sea of Galilee as well. He was one of the wealthiest men in the city and its most despised citizen.

By contrast, Jesus of Nazareth was easily their best-known and best-loved resident. Great crowds had been following him from the entire region. He had astounded them with his teaching, healed their sick, and calmed their storms.

Imagine the shock that went through the community when this great man of God called the despised tax collector to join his group of disciples (Matthew 9:9). And imagine Matthew's shock at being the one invited.

In the moment of his decision to follow Jesus, Matthew abandoned his career and with it his wealth and the protection of the Roman Empire. We could say that, of all of Jesus' apostles, Matthew gave up the most to follow his Lord. But he knew that he had been forgiven much, and he responded to that grace with the devotion of his life (Luke 7:47).

What we can learn from Matthew is that when people "turn from their wicked ways" (2 Chronicles 7:14), they turn *to* their gracious Lord. May the same be true for us today: as we turn from our own sin and selfish ways, let us turn toward the love and grace of our father.

GUIDED PRAYER

1. Meditate on the grace of God to forgive sinners like us, no matter the extent of our sins.

"The Word became flesh and dwelt among us, and we have seen his glory, glory as of the only Son from the Father, full of grace and truth" (John 1:14).

2. Consider the worst sins you have committed.

If you have not confessed them before, do so now. If you have, receive his astounding and transforming grace.

- "In him we have redemption through his blood, the forgiveness of our trespasses, according to the riches of his grace" (Ephesians 1:7).

3. Like Matthew, choose to follow your Lord fully and unconditionally today in gratitude for his all-forgiving love.

- "You did not choose me, but I chose you and appointed you that you should go and bear fruit and that your fruit should abide" (John 15:16).

GO

When Matthew chose to follow Jesus, he then invited his fellow tax collectors to meet his Lord: Matthew 9:10 says, "As Jesus reclined at table in the house, behold, many tax collectors and sinners came and were reclining with Jesus and his disciples." When we receive a gift, we want to share it. When we learn that God can and will forgive our sins, we should want others to experience the same forgiveness.

The best missionary to tax collectors was a tax collector. The best person to help an alcoholic is a recovering alcoholic. What sins and failures have you been forgiven for? How can you help someone who is where you have been?

Extended reading: Matthew 9

WEDNESDAY

Crucified upside down

—

"Jesus said to Simon Peter, 'Simon, son of John, do you love me more than these?' He said to him, 'Yes, Lord; you know that I love you.' He said to him, 'Feed my lambs.'" —John 21:15

DAY 3

One of the character traits I most admire about the apostle Peter is his transparency.

According to early tradition, the Gospel of Mark was based primarily on Peter's eyewitness testimony. In Mark 14 we read of one of Peter's greatest failures, a story he obviously shared with Mark and, through him, with the world.

It begins with Jesus' warning to his disciples in Mark 14:27, "You will all fall away." Peter responded: "Even though they all fall away, I will not" (v. 29). Jesus assured him, "Truly, I tell you, this very night, before the rooster crows twice, you will deny me three times" (v. 30). But Peter was convinced that Jesus was wrong: "He said emphatically, 'If I must die with you, I will not deny you'" (v. 31).

Of course, we know what happened that same night as Peter denied his Lord three times (Mark 14:66–72).

Fast-forward to Jesus' resurrection. He has appeared to his disciples, Peter included. He has shown them his crucified and risen body, then he came for his fallen disciple beside the Sea of Galilee where the fisherman had lived his life and made his living. John 21:15 says, "When they had finished breakfast, Jesus said to Simon Peter, 'Simon, son of John, do you love me more than these?' He said to him, 'Yes, Lord; you know that I love you.' He said to him, 'Feed my lambs.'"

Jesus repeated his question three times, and Peter gave the same answer three times. Then Jesus warned him: "Truly, truly, I say to you, when you were young, you used to dress yourself and walk wherever you wanted, but when you are old, you will stretch out your hands, and another will dress you and carry you where you do not want to go" (v. 18). John explained: "This he said to show by what kind of death he was to glorify God" (v. 19).

The story ends with this: "And after saying this he said to him, 'Follow me'" (v. 19b). And Peter did.

This fallen and now-restored disciple preached the first sermon in Christian history at Pentecost in Acts 2. He and John were used to heal a man lame from birth in Acts 3 and to preach to the crowds that responded in amazement in Acts 3–4. He would stand before the Sanhedrin with incredible courage and grace in Acts 4–5. He would be used in miraculous ways across the Roman Empire and write two epistles that are part of our New Testament.

Then, according to early tradition from a letter known as 1 Clement, the time came for him to die as Jesus had predicted: "Peter, who because of unrighteous jealousy suffered not one or two but many trials, and having thus given his testimony went to the glorious place which was his due." In his work titled *Ecclesiastical History*, the early historian Eusebius records that Peter "was crucified head-downwards; for he had requested that he might suffer in this way."

When God's people truly "turn from their wicked ways," like we read in 2 Chronicles 7:14, the Lord restores us to his kingdom purposes and redeems even our failures for his greatest glory and our greatest good. Peter is proof.

GUIDED PRAYER

1. Meditate on God's desire to forgive every sinner for every sin.

- "This is the blood of my covenant, which is poured out for many for the forgiveness of sins" (Matthew 26:28).

2. Consider the ways he redeems those who turn to him by faith.

Reflect on stories of such redemption throughout Scripture and thank God that he is redeeming your story as well.

- "He said to me, 'My grace is sufficient for you, for my power is made perfect in weakness.' Therefore I will boast all the more gladly of my weaknesses, so that the power of Christ may rest upon me" (2 Corinthians 12:9).

3. Look for ways today to share God's redeeming grace through your story and ministry.

- "One thing I do know, that though I was blind, now I see" (John 9:25).

GO

According to an early document called *Acts of the Holy Apostles Peter and Paul*, Peter chose to die as he did for this reason: "My cross ought to be fixed downmost, so as to direct my feet towards heaven; for I am not worthy to be crucified like my Lord." So "having reversed the cross, they nailed his feet up."

Extended reading: John 21

THURSDAY

A sermon I've never forgotten

—

"His father saw him and felt compassion, and ran and embraced him and kissed him." —Luke 15:20

DAY 4

I went to college at a Baptist university. One day, I heard a visiting pastor speak in chapel on the parable of the prodigal son from Luke 15:11–32.

As a religion major, I thought I knew all there was to know about this famous story. I knew that a son asking for his inheritance before his father had died was extremely disrespectful in Jesus' culture, or any culture for that matter. I knew that a Jewish boy feeding pigs was the absolute worst outcome you could imagine in their day. I knew that the father's decision to give his returning prodigal the "best robe," a "ring on his hand," and "shoes on his feet" (Luke 15:22) was a sign that the father was welcoming him not as a servant but as a son.

And I knew that the older brother who was angry and refused to go into the celebration that ensued represented the Jewish religious leaders and their condemnation of all who did not share their legalistic righteousness.

As the pastor told the story and explained these details, I waited for the sermon to be over so I could get on with my day. But when he was done, he asked a question I had never considered, one that struck me deeply and resonates with me still.

He looked at the chapel filled with college students and asked, "If you were the prodigal son, who would you want to greet you when you returned home: the loving father or the older brother?"

How would you answer his question?

Here's the good news: your Father will never be the older brother. He forgives every sin you confess and then forgets what he forgives. But here's the catch: he can receive you by grace only when you come to him for grace. He honors the freedom he has entrusted to us and will not force us to receive his gifts of love. He knocks at the door of our hearts and will come in only when we open it (Revelation 3:20). Just like the prodigal son, we have to turn toward the Father.

In Isaiah 30:18, the prophet explained: "The Lord must wait for you to come to him so he can show you his love and compassion" (NLT).

As we focus this week on God's call for his people to "turn from their wicked ways," know that when you do, you will be met by a Father who loves you more deeply than you can imagine.

When you take the first step to him, he will take all the rest to you.

Turn toward your loving father today as we enter a time of guided prayer.

GUIDED PRAYER

1. Think about Jesus' parable of the prodigal son.

Imagine yourself as the prodigal and then as the older brother. Which resonates more deeply with you today?

2. Reflect on times your Father has forgiven your sins and welcomed you home as his child.

- "By grace you have been saved through faith. And this is not your own doing; it is the gift of God, not a result of works, so that no one may boast" (Ephesians 2:8–9).

3. Ask the Spirit to show you anything in your life that displeases your Father today.

Confess what comes to your thoughts and claim his forgiving grace. Feel yourself in his loving embrace and express to him your gratitude for his grace.

- "The Lord is not slow to fulfill his promise as some count slowness, but is patient toward you, not wishing that any should perish, but that all should reach repentance" (2 Peter 3:9).

GO

Jesus' parable ends with the older brother standing outside the house where the younger brother's return is being celebrated. We're not told whether the older brother joined the party or not. But I believe Jesus ended the story like this to show us that we can decide how his story will end in our own lives.

Extended reading: Luke 15

"His father saw him and felt compassion, and ran and embraced him and kissed him."

LUKE 15:20

FRIDAY

Praying for "the gift of tears"

—

"I am Jesus, whom you are persecuting. But rise and enter the city, and you will be told what you are to do" (Acts 9:5-6).

DAY 5

The most famous conversion in Christian history began in the unlikeliest of ways.

Saul of Tarsus had been a student of Gamaliel, one of the most famous rabbis of the day, and a member of the Pharisees, the most respected religious group in the land. When the Christian movement began, Saul judged its followers to be heretics worthy of prison and even death. After he approved of Stephen's martyrdom in Acts 8:1, he set out to arrest Christians in Damascus, a major city 150 miles to the north.

On the way, he met the very One whose followers he had been violently persecuting. And as a result, Saul (his Jewish name) eventually became known as Paul (his Roman name), the greatest missionary, evangelist, and theologian in Christian history.

We might think that his astounding achievements—planting churches across the Roman Empire, writing nearly half of the New Testament, and frequently risking his life for the gospel—would outweigh his misguided persecution of Christians prior to meeting Christ. But the Apostle disagreed.

When he told the story of his conversion, he confessed his sins against Christ and his church. He said of himself in 1 Corinthians 15:9, "I am the least of the apostles, unworthy to be called an apostle, because I persecuted the church of God." He even called himself the "worst sinner of all" in 1 Timothy 1:15 (NIRV).

But why would a man who knew that his sins had been forgiven continue to recount his past failings like that? Why would he view himself with such guilt and remorse? Paul is Exhibit A of what genuine repentance looks like. When God's people "turn from their wicked ways" as we've been exploring in 2 Chronicles 7:14, we are then able to see these "ways" as God sees them. In the light of his holiness, we can view our sins far more accurately than in the darkness of temptation.

When we have an authentic experience with God's convicting Spirit and unmerited grace, we can't help but see ourselves and our sins differently. As with Isaiah before God's holiness in Isaiah 6:5, we will recognize that we are "lost" apart from his forgiveness. Our grief over our sin will then position us to experience the full depth of his mercy and love.

In My Utmost for His Highest, Oswald Chambers wrote: "The old Puritans used to pray for 'the gift of tears.' If ever you cease to know the virtue of repentance, you are in darkness. Examine yourself and see if you have forgotten how to be sorry."

Notes

Would you pray for this gift?

Let God's kindness and love lead you into the beauty of repentance today as we begin a time of guided prayer.

GUIDED PRAYER

1. Think about the story of Paul's conversion.

Hear Jesus' voice calling, "Saul, Saul, why are you persecuting me?" (Acts 9:4). Now substitute your name for that of Saul. Ask the Spirit to show you any reasons why you need to spend time in repentance today.

- "I have not come to call the righteous but sinners to repentance" (Luke 5:32).

2. Ask the Spirit to help you see your sins as God sees them.

Pray for the "gift of tears" to feel the grief that leads to genuine repentance.

- "I rejoice, not because you were grieved, but because you were grieved into repenting. For you felt a godly grief" (2 Corinthians 7:9).

3. Now confess all that is on your heart and receive your Father's forgiveness and grace.

- "Those whom I love, I reprove and discipline, so be zealous and repent" (Revelation 3:19).

GO

Martin Luther observed, "To do so no more is the truest repentance." His reflection mirrored the call of Jesus in Matthew 3:8: "Bear fruit in keeping with repentance."

One type of "fruit" that results from repentance is the desire to help others experience the same grace that has liberated us. Do you know someone who needs to experience such conviction? Or someone who doesn't have a personal relationship with Christ? Or maybe someone who is living in the blindness of sin?

Will you pray for them by name today? And will you then follow Paul's example by sharing your story with them?

Extended reading: Acts 9

SATURDAY

"Create in me a clean heart"

"Have mercy on me, O God, according to your steadfast love; according to your abundant mercy blot out my transgressions." —Psalm 51:1

DAY 6

In 2 Samuel 11, King David has a scandalous affair with a woman named Bathsheba. She was the wife of Uriah, one of David's elite military commanders. When she became pregnant, David attempted a cover-up by having Uriah killed and taking the widowed Bathsheba as his wife.

So why would someone God calls "a man after my heart" in Acts 13:22 commit such heinous sins? For the same reasons we do: we have inherited a sin nature and face the temptations and deceptions of Satan. And on top of that, according to James 1:14–15, we also choose to sin of our own free will.

What separates David from most of us is not the reality of his sin but the faith of his response.

After Nathan exposed David's immorality in 2 Samuel 12:1–12, David responded, "I have sinned against the LORD" (v. 13). Then he wrote Psalm 51 to express his contrition to God.

Rather than shutting God out, he turned to the Lord, seeking his "mercy" and appealing to his "steadfast love" (v. 1). He prayed in Psalm 51:1–2 that God would "blot out my transgressions," "wash me thoroughly from my iniquity," and "cleanse me from my sin!"

Later he prayed that the Lord would "purge me with hyssop, and I shall be clean; wash me, and I shall be whiter than snow" (v. 7). He believed that God could "let me hear joy and gladness" and "let the bones that you have broken rejoice" (v. 8). Then he prayed that God would "hide your face from my sins, and blot out all my iniquities," "create in me a clean heart," and "renew a right spirit within me" (vv. 9–10).

David believed that, in answer to his repentance, God would restore the joy of his salvation and uphold him with a willing spirit (v. 12). In fact, he was confident that he would be restored so fully that he would then teach other sinners to return to God (v. 13).

We have focused this week on God's call to his people to "turn from their wicked ways" in 2 Chronicles 7:14. Let's finish the week by claiming his amazing grace when we do. Let's believe with David that, no matter the depth and depravity of our failures, God's love and mercy are deeper and stronger still. Let's confess our sins in full faith that God will "cleanse us from *all* unrighteousness" (1 John 1:9, my emphasis) and "remember [our] sin no more" (Jeremiah 31:34).

The great preacher John Claypool told of a priest who committed a terrible sin in seminary. Though he had confessed his failure to the Lord, he lived for years with the aftermath of guilt.

One day a member of his church came to him with the startling news that the Lord had begun speaking audibly to her in prayer. The priest was dubious and said to her, "The next time the Lord speaks to you, ask him what sin your priest committed in seminary." She said she would.

She came back a few days later and the priest asked if she had done what he suggested. She said she had in fact asked the Lord what sin he had committed when he was in seminary. He asked if the Lord responded to her. She said that he did.

"What did he say?" the priest asked.

She replied, "He said, 'I don't remember.'"

How amazing is it that God extends his cleansing grace to us today? Let's reflect on this truth as we enter a time of guided prayer.

GUIDED PRAYER

1. Reflect on the story of David, Bathsheba, and Uriah.

Feel the weight of David's horrible sins. Then ask the Holy Spirit to help you respond to the biblical question, "Have you not sins of your own against the LORD your God?" (2 Chronicles 28:10).

- "Whoever knows the right thing to do and fails to do it, for him it is sin" (James 4:17).

2. Confess the sins the Spirit shows you and claim God's cleansing love.

- "As far as the east is from the west, so far does he remove our transgressions from us" (Psalm 103:12).

3. Thank God for his restoring grace in your life.

- "Let us then with confidence draw near to the throne of grace, that we may receive mercy and find grace to help in time of need" (Hebrews 4:16).

GO

Cancer survivors can encourage cancer patients in ways no one else can. Those who have lost a loved one can uniquely help those who are grieving.

In the same way, forgiven sinners can especially help other sinners find forgiveness. After David confessed his sin and experienced God's grace, he wanted to share with others the gift he had received. His example asks the question: Is repentance truly sincere if the repentant person does not then seek to help others experience repentance?

Who will be drawn closer to our Father's forgiving love through you today?

Extended reading: Psalm 51

SUNDAY

Reflection

DAY 7

As we conclude this week's focus on repentance, spend today reflecting on what the Lord has taught you.

We began by discussing how true repentance requires taking responsibility for our sins and then humbly turning away from them. From there, we examined the need not only to turn from sin but to turn from sin to God before looking at the ways in which that repentance positions us to be used by the Lord in truly amazing ways.

Next, we turned to the parable of the prodigal son for a reminder that, when we repent, God is always faithful to forgive us. However, we must be careful not to let that assurance of the Lord's forgiveness minimize our awareness of how detrimental our sins are to a strong walk with God.

Lastly, yesterday we looked to the example of David for a reminder that one of the ways in which God will often redeem our sin is by using us to help others seek repentance and find forgiveness in their own struggles.

So as we finish for today, take some time to ask the Lord if there are any sins in your life of which you need to repent. But when you make that request of God, be sure that you are ready for what he shows you. And when the Holy Spirit brings sins to mind, resist the urge to rationalize them or shift the blame to someone else. Own up to your mistakes and know that God is ready to forgive if you are ready to truly repent.

"Repent therefore, and turn back, that your sins may be blotted out, that times of refreshing may come from the presence of the Lord."

ACTS 3:19-20

WEEK SIX

Trust

MONDAY

The resolution your heart wants to make

—

"If anyone is in Christ, he is a new creation. The old has passed away; behold, the new has come." —2 Corinthians 5:17

DAY 1

In many ways, the Lenten season is like a second New Year's Day for believers. It's a time for self-reflection and renewed dedication to the Lord. But just as our New Year's resolutions tend to fade over time, it doesn't take long for life to make keeping that focus difficult as well. If we truly desire to see the kind of awakening we've discussed over the last five weeks, however, we cannot allow that commitment to waver.

With that in mind, let's take today as an opportunity to renew that commitment to drawing closer to God as we draw closer to the anniversary of Christ's death and resurrection. And the first step is understanding to what we should be committed.

Many years ago, I came across Bob Buford's bestselling book, *Halftime: Changing Your Game Plan from Success to Significance*. That was the first time I understood the difference between the two. Success is for now; significance is forever. Success is fleeting; significance is transcendent.

You and I were made for significance. We were made to outlive ourselves, to leave a legacy beyond ourselves. There is something in us that wants our days to matter when they're done. But there's only one pathway to true significance.

The apostle Paul declared, "If anyone is in Christ, he is a new creation. The old has passed away; behold, the new has come" (2 Corinthians 5:17). This promise is for you—no matter the guilt you may carry from the past, challenges you face in the present, or the fears you have for the future.

The moment you choose to be "in Christ," which means to have a personal relationship with Jesus as your Lord and Savior, you become a "new creation." You are "born again," as Jesus said in John 3:3.

Now you have the honor of helping someone else experience the same grace. God made you for this simple purpose: to know Christ and to make him known. Everything else is a means to this end.

There is nothing you can do to make God love you any more than he already does. But there's a catch: this gift of God must be received. Like Christmas presents under the tree, the gift of salvation must be opened.

Have you opened your gift yet? Are you a "new creation"? Have you been "born again"? Do you remember the day when you asked Jesus to forgive your sins and failures and turned your life over to him as your Savior and Lord?

If not, why not today?

Notes

If you are a new creation in Christ, begin by seeking to know him and to make him known. Allow his presence and his word to heal and transform you as you get to know him more deeply this year. This is the path to true significance.

And it's the resolution your heart most wants to make today.

GUIDED PRAYER

1. Meditate on the gift of this Lenten season.

Allow God's word to stir in you gratitude for the gift of life:

- "Every good gift and every perfect gift is from above, coming down from the Father of lights, with whom there is no variation or shadow due to change" (James 1:17)

2. If you are not certain you have trusted in Christ as your Savior, make this commitment now.

And if you have, reaffirm your trust in him today. There is no one prayer you must pray to become a Christian, but if you pray these words from your heart, God will hear you and make you a new creation.

- "Dear Lord, thank you for loving me. Thank you that Jesus died on the cross to pay for my sins. I turn from them now and ask you to forgive me for them. I give my life to you, trusting you as my Lord and Savior. I will live for you as long as I live. Thank you for hearing me and for making me your child today."

And if you prayed this prayer for the first time, please share this wonderful news with a Christian friend so they can help you find a church family and grow in your new faith.

3. Surrender your life and this Lenten season to God's leadership.

Ask him to guide your life each day and to use you to make him known to the world.

- "Whether you eat or drink, or whatever you do, do all to the glory of God" (1 Corinthians 10:31).

GO

When you receive a special gift, you want to share the news. Eternal life is, of course, the greatest gift of all.

Do you know someone who, to your knowledge, does not have a personal salvation relationship with Jesus? Would you begin praying for them by name? Would you share your faith story with them?

Changed lives change lives. Knowing Christ and making him known is the greatest privilege. Resolve to get to know God more deeply.

Extended reading: John 3

TUESDAY

When you can't trace his hand, trust his heart

—

"I know the plans I have for you, declares the L‌ord, plans for welfare and not for evil, to give you a future and a hope." —Jeremiah 29:11

DAY 2

As we focus this week on practical ways to place our attention on God, let's pause today to ask an honest question: Why should we *want* to trust our lives to him?

My father fought in World War II and experienced such atrocities that he never attended church again. And over many years of my own ministry, I have met many people like my dad. Their questioning is only natural since Christians believe in an all-knowing, all-loving, and all-powerful God. Because of that, he knows all about our problems, he loves us enough to help us with them, and he is powerful enough to do so.

And yet you and I live in a fallen, broken world.

If you're like me, God has not answered all your prayers in the way you wanted. Philip Yancey's book, *Disappointment with God*, was a bestseller because it spoke of what many of us have felt at times: disappointed.

Where has God disappointed you?

The first audience of today's Scripture shared our struggle. They were exiles in Babylon, living as slaves to an enemy that had stolen them from their homes and destroyed their temple.

And yet, in the midst of their suffering, their Lord promised them that he had "plans for welfare and not for evil, to give you a future and a hope." He fulfilled those plans when he raised up the Persian Empire to destroy the Babylonian Empire and return his people to their promised land. There they would rebuild their temple and reestablish their nation. Five centuries later, their Messiah would teach in that same temple and lay down his life for their sins and ours.

But how does the Bible connect God's "plans for welfare" with the evil and suffering we experience? Here are some approaches:

- Many of our problems result from our misused freedom, not God's intention (Galatians 5:13).

- The Lord uses suffering to grow us spiritually (James 1:2–4).

- We will understand more in the future than we can in the present (1 Corinthians 13:12).

- God walks with us through our hardest days (Isaiah 43:2–3).

Whichever approach is most relevant for you today, here's the reality: *the harder it is to trust God, the more we need to trust him.*

On our most painful days, when we are most tempted to turn from him, we most need his help. The sicker the patient, the more urgent the physician.

What are your greatest challenges today? What fears or worries are burdening your heart?

Spend some time naming them, and then trust them to your Lord. Remember that no matter your circumstances and challenges, he wants an "abundant," joy-filled, transformed life for you.

In his book *The Promised Land,* nineteenth-century Scottish minister John MacDuff was right: when you can't trace God's hand, trust his heart.

GUIDED PRAYER

1. Identify a way you are disappointed with God today.

Be specific and honest.

- "Why, O Lord, do you stand far away? Why do you hide yourself in times of trouble?" (Psalm 10:1).

2. Ask him for the faith to trust him with your problem.

When we lack faith, we can pray for the faith to have faith.

- "I believe; help my unbelief!" (Mark 9:24)

3. Trust your challenges and your day to your Father's providential plan and love.

- "Delight yourself in the Lord, and he will give you the desires of your heart. Commit your way to the Lord; trust in him, and he will act. He will bring forth your righteousness as the light, and your justice as the noonday" (Psalm 37:4–6).

GO

Henri Nouwen made popular the concept of the "wounded healer," the person who helps others with the same struggles they have experienced personally. For example, after my father died when I was in college, a friend whose father had died a few months earlier gave me words of wisdom I remember to this day. When our oldest son had cancer, cancer survivors were among our greatest encouragers.

As you trust God with your hard places this year, look for ways you can serve others facing similar challenges. Remember: God "comforts us in all our affliction, so that we may be able to comfort those who are in any affliction, with the comfort with which we ourselves are comforted by God" (2 Corinthians 1:4)

How can you share the comfort you have received today?

Extended reading: Jeremiah 29:1–14

WEDNESDAY

God redeems all he allows

—

"We know that for those who love God all things work together for good, for those who are called according to his purpose. For those whom he foreknew he also predestined to be conformed to the image of his Son, in order that he might be the firstborn among many brothers." —Romans 8:28–29

DAY 3

In 1945, a group of starving children was rescued from a Nazi concentration camp. Allied soldiers fed and clothed them, but the children still struggled to sleep at night. They were restless, fearful, and agitated. The soldiers could not understand why until a counselor suggested that they give the children a slice of bread to take with them to bed—not to eat, just to hold.

With this tangible promise that they would have food for the next day, the children slept soundly.

What is your greatest fear for the future?

I could list several. So, as we look at trusting the Lord with this day, let's focus on this promise: *God redeems all he allows.*

Your omniscient Father knows all of the problems you face and assures you, as our Scripture states, that "in all things, God things work together for good." This phrase, in its original Greek language, could be literally translated as "every event in your life will cooperate with every other dimension of your life for your benefit."

Here's the reason God is working through "all things:" It's so that we will be "conformed to the image of his Son." He uses every dimension of our lives to make us more like Jesus.

And in this way, God redeems all he allows.

Let's unpack this fact just a bit more.

Matthew 10:29 explains that because the Lord is sovereign, he must allow or cause all that happens in our world. His allowing certain things shouldn't be confused with His approval of them. And, because "God is love" as stated in 1 John 4:8, he can only want our best. Lastly, because he is "holy," as the Scriptures mention, for example, in Isaiah 6:3, he can never make a mistake.

However, God *would* be making a mistake if he allowed or caused *anything* that he did not redeem for a greater good in this world and/or the next. Since he cannot make a mistake, his character requires him to redeem all he allows for the purpose of making us more like Jesus.

To be clear: this doesn't mean we will always understand God's redemption in this world. I don't fully understand the airplanes I fly on or even the phone I use every single day. But one day you and I *will* understand what we cannot comprehend today (1 Corinthians 13:12).

Another challenging truth is that not *everyone* experiences God's redemption. Those who reject his word are still used to accomplish his will, though they miss out on the benefits they would have experienced through obedience. In Exodus, we see how God used Pharaoh's "hardened

Notes

heart" to liberate the Jewish people, though Pharaoh himself missed out on any blessing. Even in Judas' betrayal we see the Lord weaving his beautiful story of redemption and victory over sin and death.

We must have faith to receive what grace wants to give. Those who love God and want to be like his Son are the ones who most fully experience his redemptive providence in their lives.

Will you put your day in the redemptive hands of your loving Lord? If you struggle to put your faith in God, ask him to help you.

GUIDED PRAYER

1. Meditate on the fact that God's providence is redeeming every dimension of your life that you entrust to him.

- God "saved us and called us to a holy calling, not because of our works but because of his own purpose and grace, which he gave us in Christ Jesus before the ages began" (2 Timothy 1:9).

2. Ask your Father to show you how you can be more like Jesus today.

Pray that he would show you what you need to stop doing and start doing to be more like your Savior.

- "Whoever says he abides in him ought to walk in the same way in which he walked" (1 John 2:6).

3. Ask God to show you how you can partner with him in his work of redemption today.

- "We are his workmanship, created in Christ Jesus for good works, which God prepared beforehand, that we should walk in them" (Ephesians 2:10).

GO

Being like Jesus includes helping others to be like Jesus. Mark 10:45 says he came "not to be served but to serve," and he calls us to do the same (John 13:14). We must breathe out to breathe in. As we help others follow Christ, we actually become more like Christ as well.

There is no greater purpose than being like Jesus and helping others be like Jesus. But God can only lead those who will follow and will only give what we're willing to receive. Jesus' word in Revelation 3:20 to the Christians in Laodicea is his invitation to us: "Behold, I stand at the door and knock. If anyone hears my voice and opens the door, I will come in to him and eat with him, and he with me."

Will you open the door of your heart to him today? Will you help someone else do the same?

Extended reading: Romans 8

THURSDAY

"All of God there is, is in this moment"

—

"Remember not the former things, nor consider the things of old. Behold, I am doing a new thing; now it springs forth, do you not perceive it? I will make a way in the wilderness and rivers in the desert." —Isaiah 43:18–19

DAY 4

When I pastored a church, I was meeting with our new worship leader to plan the upcoming Sunday service. When we finished, I told him I wanted to sketch out plans for the next few Sundays as well. This is how I liked to operate in most of my life: create a detailed plan and check off tasks one by one. But our worship leader smiled at my request that day and said something I've never forgotten: "All of God there is, is in this moment."

Planning for what's to come is still biblical and appropriate, as Jesus reminded us in Luke 14:28. But if we live in the past or the future, we risk missing God's presence in the present.

After all, he is the Great "I Am," not the "I Was" or the "I Will Be," as he says in Exodus 3:14. His word is clear in Psalm 118:24: "*This* is the day that the Lord has made; let us rejoice and be glad in it" (emphasis added).

This is why today's verse, Isaiah 43:18, urges us to "remember not the former things, nor consider the things of old." We should learn from the past, but we are not to live there. Rather, God assures us, "I am doing a new thing." In this new day, he will "make a way in the wilderness and rivers in the desert." But we must choose to live in the present and follow him into this new way by faith.

We see the importance of this in every area of our lives.

- In our salvation: 2 Corinthians 6:2 says, "In a favorable time I listened to you, and in a day of salvation I have helped you." We have only today to prepare for eternity.

- In our worship: "Sing to the LORD a new song" exhorts Isaiah 42:10. Yesterday's worship is not sufficient for today.

- In prayer: You are probably familiar with the Lord's Prayer. In Matthew 6:11, Jesus prays "Give us this day our *daily* bread" (emphasis added). God invites us to pray for the present, not just for the past or future.

- In faith: Jesus says, in Matthew 6:34, "Do not be anxious about tomorrow, for tomorrow will be anxious for itself. Sufficient for the day is its own trouble." As Dale Carnegie noted, "Today is the tomorrow you worried about yesterday."

Walking with God means being in his will *today*. Giving God our year means giving him our day. In her book *The Writing Life*, Annie Dillard was right: "How we spend our days is, of course, how we spend our lives."

Have you fully surrendered this day to your Lord? Will you give him permission to change your plans? Those who experience God most fully are those who exercise the faith to follow him most unconditionally. Some of the best advice I've ever received came from a wise mentor to "stay faithful to the last word you heard from God and open to the next."

Notes

GUIDED PRAYER

1. Meditate on the fact that God is "doing a new thing" in your life today.

- "The steadfast love of the Lord never ceases; his mercies never come to an end; they are new every morning; great is your faithfulness" (Lamentations 3:22–23).

2. Ask him to help you trust in the future he has prepared for you.

- "Trust in the Lord with all your heart, and do not lean on your own understanding. In all your ways acknowledge him, and he will make straight your paths" (Proverbs 3:5–6).

3. Ask God to show you what plans he has for you *today*.

Trust that he will lead you where you need to go.

- "Seek first the kingdom of God and his righteousness, and all these things will be added to you" (Matthew 6:33).

GO

I often hear people ask God to "be with them." Although I understand the sentiment, this is a prayer we never actually need to pray. In Matthew 28:20 Jesus promised us, "I am with you always, to the end of the age." But it can be easy to feel as though the Lord has somehow gone missing. Oftentimes this is because we are having difficulty sensing his presence. Instead of feeling the need to ask the Lord to be present with you, try asking him to make you ever more aware of his presence.

If you know someone who is fearful for the future, you can invite them to trust in the promise from God in Isaiah

41:10, "Fear not, for I am with you; be not dismayed, for I am your God; I will strengthen you, I will help you, I will uphold you with my righteous right hand." Together, let's trust in him for the "new thing" he is doing in our world.

As you go throughout your day, let the Lord lead you to a place you've never been.

Let him use you to serve someone in a way you never have.

Let's not miss out on the incredible thing God wants to do in us and through us today.

Extended reading: Hebrews 11

FRIDAY

Eighteen inches from God

—

"Oh, taste and see that the Lord *is good! Blessed is the man who takes refuge in him!" —Psalm 34:8*

DAY 5

On the first Easter Sunday, the risen Christ joined two people on their way to Emmaus, a town seven miles west of Jerusalem. As we read the story in Luke 24:13–35, they seemed to understand a great deal about Jesus: they knew he was "a prophet mighty in deed and word before God and all the people" and that he had been crucified (v. 19). They had hoped he would be the Messiah and had even heard that he had been raised from the dead.

And yet, despite all of their knowledge, "their eyes were kept from recognizing him." They were eighteen inches from God—the distance from the head to the heart.

Not long after, when they personally heard Jesus speak biblical truth and joined him in worship, "their eyes were opened," and they finally recognized him for who he truly is. "They said to each other, 'Did not our hearts burn within us while he talked to us on the road, while he opened to us the Scriptures?'" The reality of Jesus moved from their heads to their hearts.

God is less a concept to be understood than a Person to be experienced. In his book *Men Who Met God*, A. W. Tozer reminded us: "Genuine Christian experience must always include an encounter with God."

As we focus this week on learning to walk in faith, let's resolve today to *experience* him every day. Psalm 34:8, our verse for today, is God's invitation: "Oh, taste and see that the Lord is good! Blessed is the man who takes refuge in him!"

Connecting with God in a meaningful way can actually be challenging for those of us who meet with God using devotionals like this one. We can assume that because we are making time for God, we must be experiencing God. However, as I have learned personally over the years, our heads and our hearts are only as connected as we choose for them to be. If we're not careful, it's possible we could learn more about God without truly experiencing his love.

So how can we experience God in a transforming way every day?

- First, we must meet him in his word: Hebrews 4:12 reminds us, "The word of God is living and active, sharper than any two-edged sword, piercing to the division of soul and of spirit, of joints and of marrow, and discerning the thoughts and intentions of the heart." God longs to speak to our hearts through his word.

- Connect with God in prayer: Philippians 4:6 says, "Do not be anxious about *anything*, but in *everything* by prayer and supplication with thanksgiving let your requests be made known to God" (my emphasis).

- Listen for his voice in his creation: Psalm 19:1 puts it this way, "The heavens declare the glory of God, and the sky above proclaims his handiwork."

- Engage in deep relationships with other believers: Proverbs 27:17 says, "Iron sharpens iron, and one man sharpens another."

Francis Schaeffer was right when he titled one of his books *He Is There, and He Is Not Silent*. God is with you right now and desires to connect with your heart. Will you listen for his voice and experience his transforming presence today?

GUIDED PRAYER

1. Meditate on the fact that God wants to speak to you today.

- "My sheep hear my voice, and I know them, and they follow me" (John 10:27).

2. Make time to hear his voice in Scripture, prayer, and worship.

As you read the following verse, ask the Spirit to speak through it to you. If you can, write down the thoughts that come to your mind and respond to God with gratitude and praise.

- "Your word is a lamp to my feet and a light to my path" (Psalm 119:105).

3. Spend time dwelling on the truth that God is your refuge today.

Ask God to help you walk in the life that he intends for you today.

- "Trust in him at all times, O people; pour out your heart before him; God is a refuge for us" (Psalm 62:8).

GO

The time to seek intimacy with God is before we even recognize we need more intimacy. When the rain starts, it's too late to go home for an umbrella. When an enemy surrounds us, it's too late to run to the fortress.

Choose to make God your refuge today. Then ask yourself: Who do I know who needs to do the same?

Invite them to claim your Father's promises in the Psalms, "This God—his way is perfect; the word of the LORD proves true; he is a shield for all those who take refuge in him" (Psalm 18:30). When you draw close to him, "under his wings you will find refuge" (Psalm 91:4).

Will you live "under his wings" today?

Extended reading: Psalm 91

SATURDAY

Your spiritual alarm clock

—

"You know the time, that the hour has come for you to wake from sleep. For salvation is nearer to us now than when we first believed. The night is far gone; the day is at hand. So then let us cast off the works of darkness and put on the armor of light." —Romans 13:11-12

DAY 6

In our Scripture today, Paul testifies that "the hour has come for you to wake from sleep." "Sleep" in this context refers to spiritual lethargy, an attitude or lifestyle of complacent apathy. And here's why they should "wake from sleep": "Salvation is nearer to us now than when we first believed."

Paul then extends his metaphor in verse 12: "The night is far gone; the day is at hand. So then let us cast off the works of darkness and put on the armor of light." He's referring to the weapons of spiritual warfare, such as truth, righteousness, the gospel of peace, faith, salvation, Scripture, and prayer, which he elaborates on in his letter to the Ephesians.

Just as Paul wrote to the Christians in Rome: we have only today to be ready for eternity. I learned this in a vivid way many years ago.

One Sunday morning, I shared a message on the topic of judgment and the need to be ready today. Following our evening service that same night, an elderly couple stopped to thank me for my message that morning. They told me they'd taken my words to heart and made time that afternoon to pray together, confessing their sins and preparing to meet the Lord one day.

The next day, the wife passed away from a heart attack.

The day after her passing, I received a thank-you note she'd written on that Sunday afternoon and had put in her mailbox in case she didn't see me that night at church. I received it on Tuesday and read it at her memorial service on Wednesday. I still have that letter to this day.

I share all of this not to scare or sadden us but simply as an important reminder. No one knows when Jesus will return, but we do know this: we are all one day closer to eternity than ever before.

Let us live like it could be today.

GUIDED PRAYER

1. Meditate on the brevity of life and the urgency of living for Christ.

- "Seek the LORD while he may be found; call upon him while he is near" (Isaiah 55:6).

2. Ask the Holy Spirit to help you prepare to meet God face-to-face.

Ask him to bring to your mind anything in your life that is grieving your Father, then confess all that comes to your thoughts. Receive his forgiveness, and ask him to help you live today and every day with repentance and godliness.

- "If we confess our sins, he is faithful and just to forgive us our sins and to cleanse us from all unrighteousness" (1 John 1:9).

3. Think about how you would live today if it were your last.

What things would matter most? What wouldn't matter at all?

- "As we have opportunity, let us do good to everyone" (Galatians 6:10).

GO

If you knew the Lord would return tomorrow, what would you change today? Would you seek forgiveness from someone? Would you forgive someone? Would you stop doing something? Would you start doing something?

Even if you knew you had another thirty years to live, living with this sense of urgency leads us to a life of fruitfulness and joy. Living for heaven is the best way to live on earth. Imagine a culture in which everyone did the same.

In light of the urgency of Jesus' return, would you join me in praying for a spiritual awakening?

In Matthew 24:45–46, Jesus taught us, "Who then is the faithful and wise servant, whom his master has set over his household, to give them their food at the proper time? Blessed is that servant whom his master will find so doing when he comes."

Will you be "blessed" today?

Extended reading: Psalm 31

"*Seek the Lord while he may be found; call upon him while he is near.*"

—ISAIAH 55:6

WEEK SEVEN:
HOLY WEEK

Prepare

PALM SUNDAY

Don't join the crowd

—

"For Christ also suffered once for sins, the righteous for the unrighteous, that he might bring us to God." —1 Peter 3:18

DAY 1

Over the last six weeks, we've discussed what it looks like to trust God and pursue the kind of honest and devoted relationship with him that he desires of us. A key element of entering into that relationship, however, is embracing who God is rather than who we wish he would be. And few times in Scripture was this conflict between our desires and the Lord's more clearly laid out than on Palm Sunday.

By most historical reckonings, it was Sunday, April 12, in the year 29 AD when Jesus of Nazareth rode a donkey into Jerusalem.

A "great" crowd of Jews has come from all over the world for the Passover Feast; some ancient historians number them at more than two million.

Now they have "heard that Jesus was on his way to Jerusalem." They have heard the stories: how he healed the man born blind, and the leper and the paralytic, and raised Lazarus from the dead. For generations they have been taught to pray for their Messiah, the Promised One of God who would liberate his people from their cursed oppressors and establish their nation on earth. Now they believe that their prayers have been answered.

So the crowds went out to meet him, shouting "Hosanna! Blessed is he who comes in the name of the Lord, even the King of Israel!" (John 12:13).

This is the One who would overthrow Pilate and Caesar, drive the cursed Roman soldiers from their streets and cities, and establish the great Jewish nation for all time.

God was finally going to answer their prayers the way they asked him to. He was finally going to give them what they wanted. He was going to meet their needs. But when he didn't, how long did their adoration last? How long before "Hosanna!" turned to "Crucify!"?

Jesus knew that they had it all wrong, that the Messiah they wanted was not the Messiah they needed. But that mistake was hardly limited to the crowds that lined the street on that fateful morning. If we're not careful, you and I can make the same mistake today.

GUIDED PRAYER

1. Palm branches were symbols of victory in the ancient world, but they did not grow in Jerusalem. Rather, people brought them from the surrounding areas. **Reflect on what that says about the mindset of the people who welcomed Jesus that day.**

Ask the Lord to help you recognize if there are any areas of your life where your excitement for who you want Jesus to be has made it difficult to understand who he actually is.

2. "Hosanna" means "save us, we pray." How would you describe the salvation that the people were looking for that day? How does it compare to the relationship you have with Christ?

3. Close your time by asking God to help you identify any ways in which your understanding of who he is diverges from the truth of Scripture.

GO

Have you been part of the Palm Sunday crowd lately? A fan in the stands, coming to watch your team win? It's human nature to join them, to come to God for what we want him to do for us.

It can be tempting at times to go to church for what we can get out of it. To worship in order to be inspired, encouraged, or uplifted. To listen for advice on handling time or stress or marriage or family. To serve to be noticed. To shout "Hosanna!" so long as the Nazarene does what we want, and "Crucify!" if he does not.

All the while, the One who came on Palm Sunday and died on Good Friday deserves our worship not for what he will do for us, but for what he has done. Not so he will love us, but because he does. Not so he will bless us, but because he has. Not so he will give us what we want, but because he has already given us all that we need. At the cost of his own tortured, horrific, innocent execution, dying on our cross for our sins.

As we draw closer to Easter this week, let's also make sure we're drawing closer to the real Christ rather than one of our own making.

Extended reading: Psalm 27

"For Christ also suffered once for sins, the righteous for the unrighteous, that he might bring us to God."

1 PETER 3:18

MONDAY

You are God's temple

—

"Let us then with confidence draw near to the throne of grace, that we may receive mercy and find grace to help in time of need." —Hebrews 4:16

DAY 2

Do you sometimes feel unworthy to come to God?

Well, there is good news for you today, this first day of Holy Week.

After announcing himself to the crowds as the Messiah on Palm Sunday, Jesus returned to the suburb of Bethany for the night. The very next morning, he and his disciples walked back into the Holy City and into the temple.

When they arrived, Jesus found money changers charging exorbitant rates to convert Roman money into the currency required for the annual temple tax. They were also demanding unfair prices for the only sacrificial animals the priests would accept. In anger, Jesus drove these corrupt merchants from the temple.

Why was he so upset?

He explained in Mark 11:17: "Is it not written, 'My house shall be called a house of prayer for all the nations'? But you have made it a den of robbers."

The word *nations* comes from the original Greek word ethnos, which means "all races." This would include every person—regardless of nationality—being taken advantage of by the merchants. See, Jesus was making the point that God intended his temple to be a place where everyone was welcome to meet with him.

He still does.

Here's why it matters: because your Savior paid the price for your salvation, "you are God's temple" since "God's Spirit dwells in you" (1 Corinthians 3:16). Because of that truth, "Let us then with confidence draw near to the throne of grace, that we may receive mercy and find grace to help in time of need" (Hebrews 4:16, my emphasis).

You don't need to go to Jerusalem to meet with God.

His mercy and grace are available here and now.

All you must do is draw near.

Let us do that together now as we enter a time of guided prayer.

GUIDED PRAYER

1. Picture the scene as Jesus overturns the money changers' tables and releases their animals.

Is there anything he needs to remove from your "temple" so you can make it a "house of prayer" today? As he brings things to mind, confess what needs to be cleansed and receive his forgiving grace.

- Jesus "is able to save to the uttermost those who draw near to God through him" (Hebrews 7:25).

2. The word *mercy* can be defined as "not getting what we deserve" with regard to God's judgment. **Why do you need to "receive mercy" today?** Take time right now to "draw near to his throne of grace."

- "The steadfast love of the Lord never ceases; his mercies never come to an end; they are new every morning; great is your faithfulness" (Lamentations 3:22–23).

3. If mercy is "not getting what we deserve," grace is "getting what we don't deserve" with regard to God's forgiveness and provision. **Where do you need to "find grace" today?** "Draw near to the throne of grace" now.

- We "are justified by his grace as a gift, through the redemption that is in Christ Jesus" (Romans 3:24).

GO

Before I became a Christian, I thought I wouldn't be welcome in church because of my mistakes and failures. If someone from a neighborhood church had not invited me to come, I would never have taken that first step.

So as you go today, ask the Lord to put someone on your heart who needs the mercy and grace of God. He will answer your prayer. If you invite them to your church or offer to pray for them, you will plant a seed the Spirit can use to draw them to your Savior.

Max Lucado wrote, "God's mercies are new every morning. Receive them."

Then share them, to the glory of God.

Extended reading: Psalm 103

"Let us then with confidence draw near to the throne of grace, that we may receive mercy and find grace to help in time of need."

HEBREWS 4:16

TUESDAY

Are you in love with God?

—

"We love because he first loved us." —1 John 4:19

DAY 3

You won't be surprised to learn that, as a vocational minister, I would claim to love God. But I must confess: I sometimes struggle to be *in love* with God. I sometimes serve him more out of obedience than out of a deep love for my Lord. You may feel the same way.

Thankfully, there's hope for us today.

On Tuesday of Holy Week, Jesus' enemies gathered around him, looking for a way to discredit him in front of the crowds. Matthew 22:35 tells us that at some point, "one of them, a lawyer, asked him a question to test him." Test translates from a word that implies they meant to tempt or trap Jesus.

Here was his question: "Teacher, which is the greatest commandment in the Law?" (v. 36). Now this was a seemingly impossible question to answer. The Jews recognize 613 commands in their law, and if Jesus picked just one of them, they could accuse him of ignoring or minimizing the rest.

You're probably familiar with his response: "You shall love the LORD your God with all your heart and with all your soul and with all your mind" (v. 37). The "heart" in Scripture is the seat of the emotions and the will. The "soul" refers to the "breath" or "life" itself. The "mind" refers to intellect and understanding. And by answering in this way, Jesus both stunned his enemies and powerfully communicated how much God longs for relationship with us.

I sometimes feel discouraged since I know how far I fall short of loving God in all these ways. But here's a thought that helps me when I'm feeling this way: Jesus' response actually describes the way our triune God loves us.

God the Father proved that he loves us with "all his heart" when he sent his Son to die so we could live eternally.

God the Son proved that he loves us with "all his soul" when he surrendered his life to his Father's will and chose to die for our sins.

And God the Spirit proved that he loves us with "all his mind" as "the mind of the Spirit . . . intercedes for the saints according to the will of God" (Romans 8:27).

When anyone loves us, we are naturally moved to love them in response. This can be even more true of our relationship with God: "We love because he first loved us" (1 John 4:19).

So today, let's focus on God's great love for us as we enter into a time of guided prayer.

Notes

GUIDED PRAYER

1. God the Father made the decision on Good Friday to allow his Son to die for your sake. **What would you like to say to him in response?**

- "For our sake he made him to be sin who knew no sin, so that in him we might become the righteousness of God" (2 Corinthians 5:21).

2. Reflect on God the Son's decision on Maundy Thursday to remain in Gethsemane instead of run, choosing to stay and die for your sake. **What would you like to say to him in response?**

- "He himself bore our sins in his body on the tree, that we might die to sin and live to righteousness. By his wounds you have been healed" (1 Peter 2:24).

3. Reflect on God the Spirit's decision to intercede for you right now. **What would you like to say to him in response?**

- "The Spirit helps us in our weakness. For we do not know what to pray for as we ought, but the Spirit himself intercedes for us with groanings too deep for words" (Romans 8:26).

GO

When we reflect on God's love for us, we are moved to love him in response. But part of loving someone is loving those they love. For example, you cannot truly love me if you hate my family.

The second part of Jesus' response to the lawyer on this day in Holy Week was connected to the first: "You shall love your neighbor as yourself" (Matthew 22:39). And in the parable of the Good Shepherd, he defined our "neighbor" as anyone with a need we can meet (Luke 10:37).

Who is your neighbor today?

Extended reading: Psalm 86

*"We love because he
first loved us."*

1 JOHN 4:19

WEDNESDAY

Sitting at the feet of God

—

"Blessed rather are those who hear the word of God and keep it!" —Luke 11:28

DAY 4

If God could speak audibly to you right now, what would you like him to say? Are there questions you would like him to answer? Directions you wish he would give? Wisdom you need from his omniscience?

These questions seem almost facetious, don't they? Have you ever heard God speak in an audible voice? I haven't. Does this mean that God does not speak to us?

Not at all. He just doesn't always speak in the way we expect. And we also have to make time to listen.

Today is Wednesday of Holy Week. The Bible doesn't record a single event of this day. But we *do* know that Jesus was staying with his disciples at the home of Mary, Martha, and Lazarus in Bethany (a suburb of Jerusalem).

How did he spend the day?

Probably teaching his followers about tomorrow's trials, preparing them for the shock and pain they would soon face. He likely comforted his close friends on the eve of his arrest. And he prepared himself to go to the cross for us. As Jesus often prayed early in the morning (Mark 1:35) and late at night (Luke 6:12), so he spent this day in communion with his Father.

When last did you spend time listening to your King?

His Spirit speaks to us *rationally* through the words of Scripture and the use of our minds. He speaks to us *practically* through circumstances and people. He speaks to us *intuitively* as he moves in our emotions and attitudes.

The point is: God wants us to hear his voice and know his will even more than we do. We just need to make time to listen.

Let's do so as we enter into guided prayer.

GUIDED PRAYER

1. Take a few moments to be alone with your Father. Visualize Jesus at Bethany surrounded by his disciples and friends, yourself among them. Picture him in the center of the room and sit at his feet.

- "Jesus entered a village. A woman named Martha welcomed him into her house. And she had a sister called Mary, who sat at the Lord's feet and listened to his teaching" (Luke 10:38–39).

2. Spend a few minutes in thanksgiving and praise. Thank him for what he did for you this Holy Week. Praise him for his love and grace. Listen for his voice in response directing you to biblical truth or speaking to your spirit.

- "Enter his gates with thanksgiving, and his courts with praise! Give thanks to him; bless his name!" (Psalm 100:4).

3. Close your time with your Father by committing to him your grateful obedience. Ask him for the next steps he intends for you. Then, if you can, journal any word you feel you heard from him. Ask him to help you obey what he has revealed to you.

- "Blessed rather are those who hear the word of God and keep it!" (Luke 11:28).

GO

Listening to God is a vital part of knowing God as we love him with all our heart, soul, and mind. But it is also a means to the end of helping other people know him as well.

When we love Jesus by sitting at his feet and listening to his voice, he will usually show us how we are to love someone else in response. Then they will be drawn to love our Lord, hear his voice, and lead someone else to him. In this way, God's kingdom multiplies across our world.

Whom will you tell about your Savior today?

Extended reading: Luke 10:38–42

"Blessed rather are those who hear the word of God and keep it!"

LUKE 11:28

MAUNDY THURSDAY

When you question God's love for you

—

*"God shows his love for us in
that while we were still sinners,
Christ died for us." —Romans 5:8*

DAY 5

Have you ever had a moment when you wondered if God still loved you?

For me, our older son's cancer diagnosis several years ago comes to mind. I've also thought of my father's death in 1979 at the age of fifty-five. At the time, it was hard even to admit my feelings to myself. But I knew that God was able to prevent our son's cancer and my father's death, yet he didn't, so what option was left except that he chose not to?

And if he chose not to save me and my family from such heartache and pain, what does this say about his love for us?

When you question God's love, I encourage you to make your way back to Maundy Thursday. This was the night when Jesus told his best friends, "My soul is very sorrowful, even to death" (Matthew 26:38). He prayed three times that he would not have to go to the cross.

And three times his Father said no to his Son so he could say yes to you.

After saying to his Father, "Your will be done" (v. 42), Jesus then waited in the Garden of Gethsemane for the soldiers to come. He could see them as they marched out of the walls of the city of Jerusalem, down into the Kidron Valley, and up the Mount of Olives. At any point, he could have fled into the Judean wilderness and returned to Galilee out of their reach.

Instead, he watched and waited for the shame, the thorns, the whipping, and the nails he knew were coming. He chose to do all of that, for you.

This was all before you could do anything to earn or even receive his love. This was before you asked Jesus to forgive your sins and become your Lord. It was before your first act of obedience to his will.

Scripture is clear: "God shows his love for us in that while we were *still* sinners, Christ died for us" (Romans 5:8, my emphasis).

The next time you wonder if God loves you, return to Maundy Thursday.

GUIDED PRAYER

1. Is there something in your life that causes you to question God's love for you? If so, name it. Tell God about it. Ask his Spirit to help you trust his love and experience his grace.

- "See what kind of love the Father has given to us, that we should be called children of God; and so we are" (1 John 3:1).

2. Picture Jesus on Maundy Thursday in the Garden of Gethsemane. Hear him say to his Father, "Not as I will, but as you will" (Matthew 26:39). Know that he chose in that moment to die for you and that he would do it all again just for you. How would you like to respond to your Savior?

- "Greater love has no one than this, that someone lay down his life for his friends" (John 15:13).

3. Reflect on the events of that night: Jesus' arrest, his illegal trials, his humiliation before the Roman soldiers, and the scourging and crucifixion that would follow. Recognize the depth of your sins and the depth of your Savior's grace and respond with humility, contrition, and gratitude.

- "He himself bore our sins in his body on the tree, that we might die to sin and live to righteousness. By his wounds you have been healed" (1 Peter 2:24).

GO

An elderly professor once said to me, "Son, be kind to everyone, because everyone's having a hard time." Everyone you know has reasons to wonder if God loves them.

And yet one of the ways that our Father demonstrates his love for us is through his children. As you go, ask the Lord to open the door to a genuine conversation with someone you know who needs to talk about something they're facing. Then trust him to give you his heart for them and his words of healing grace.

Extended reading: Romans 10

"God shows his love for us in that while we were still sinners, Christ died for us."

ROMANS 5:8

GOOD FRIDAY

Why did Jesus have to die for you?

—

"The wages of sin is death, but the free gift of God is eternal life in Christ Jesus our Lord." —Romans 6:23

DAY 6

You probably know that Jesus died on Good Friday for our sins so we could be saved. But why couldn't God simply forgive them without the sacrifice of Jesus?

If someone owes *you* money, you don't require that a third person die to pay their debt. When someone hurts you, you can simply forgive them. In fact, you're told by Scripture to do so in Ephesians 4:32.

Why, then, did our Father not simply forgive us as he tells us to forgive others? Why did he require his Son to die so we could be forgiven?

When we look at Romans 6:23, we see that it says "the wages of sin is death." "Wages" can also be translated as "compensation" or "payment." So when we choose to sin, the ultimate payment or consequence of our choice is death.

This is because sin breaks our relationship with a holy God: Isaiah 59:2 says, "Your iniquities have made a separation between you and your God." And our relationship with God is our source of life. As Jesus said in John 10:10, "I came that they may have life and have it abundantly."

When we cut flowers from their roots and place them in a vase, at that moment they begin to die. They may look vibrant and healthy, but we have cut them off from their source of life. This is what sin does to humans.

Consequently, to pay the penalty incurred by sin, someone must die. But another person cannot die for your sins since they have their own sins for which to pay. The only person who could die for our sins would be someone who had never sinned and had no debt of his own to pay.

The only person in all of human history who qualifies is the sinless Lord Jesus.

Hebrews 4:15 says, "For we do not have a high priest who is unable to sympathize with our weaknesses, but one who in every respect has been tempted as we are, yet without sin."

This is why Jesus had to die for you. But don't forget: he made the choice to do so. We're told in Revelation 13:8 that he is "the Lamb who was slain from the creation of the world" (NIV), which means that, before time began, Jesus chose to die for you.

He would do it all again, just for you.

GUIDED PRAYER

1. Reflect on the last sin you committed. Recognize that this sin alone would be enough to separate you from a holy God and send you to an eternity in hell. Take a moment to express your gratitude to God for the sacrifice and grace of Jesus.

Notes

- "Christ also suffered once for sins, the righteous for the unrighteous, that he might bring us to God" (1 Peter 3:18).

2. Consider the depth of pain Jesus suffered when he was whipped, beaten, and executed on this day. Crucifixion is one of the cruelest forms of execution ever devised. As a result, you can face no suffering that he did not experience for you. What pain would you trust to him today?

- "He himself bore our sins in his body on the tree, that we might die to sin and live to righteousness. By his wounds you have been healed" (1 Peter 2:24).

3. Reflect on the fact that the Father watched his Son suffer unimaginable torture for you. Thank him for such unimaginable love and grace.

- "For our sake [God] made him to be sin who knew no sin, so that in him we might become the righteousness of God" (2 Corinthians 5:21).

GO

Philip Yancey observed, "Grace teaches us that God loves because of who God is, not because of who we are."

Every person you know needs to experience such grace. They need to know that they have been "died for," that someone took the penalty for their sins and purchased their salvation.

The best way to respond today to the grace of Good Friday is to share that grace with someone else.

Then today will be "Good" Friday, indeed.

Extended reading: Romans 6

"The wages of sin is death, but the free gift of God is eternal life in Christ Jesus our Lord."

ROMANS 6:23

SATURDAY

Grace is greater than guilt

—

"Blessed is the one whose transgression is forgiven, whose sin is covered." —Psalm 32:1

DAY 7

We know from 1 John 1:9 that "if we confess our sins, [God] is faithful and just to forgive us our sins and to cleanse us from all unrighteousness." We know that he then separates our sins "as far as the east is from the west" (Psalm 103:12), casts them "into the depths of the sea" (Micah 7:19), and "remembers your sins no more" (Isaiah 43:25 NIV).

Then why do we often feel guilt over what God has already forgiven?

Here's part of the problem: We don't like owing anyone, even God. We'd much rather have someone in our debt than be in theirs. And on top of that, we inherently feel that debts must be paid and wrongs put right.

Because of that, if God won't punish us for our sins, we may feel the need to punish ourselves until we feel somehow that we've paid our debt and we no longer owe God for his forgiveness. But this grieves our Father and damages our souls.

What's the answer?

Tomorrow, we'll celebrate Easter, when Jesus rose from the dead, proving that he is the divine Son of God and that his death truly did pay for our sins, purchase our salvation, and provide our eternal life. However, on this day in Holy Week, his body was still in the grave. We were without the hope of his grace. We were still trapped by our sins.

The key for each of us is to make every day, even the Saturday before Easter, Resurrection Day. The key is to meet with the risen Lord Jesus daily, give him our mistakes and failures, and receive his grace in response.

Then, when guilt attacks, we can say to it, "I have confessed that sin, my Lord has forgiven me by his grace, and grace is greater than guilt." Your guilt may come back again, and you'll have to say again, "Grace is greater than guilt." You may have to do this a hundred times today and ninety times tomorrow. But eventually your guilt will leave and you will be free.

First John 3:19–20 says, "By this we shall know that we are of the truth and reassure our heart before him; for whenever our heart condemns us, God is greater than our heart, and he knows everything."

It's a fact that can change our lives: grace is greater than guilt.

GUIDED PRAYER

1. Are you struggling with guilt today? Name your guilt, specifically and honestly. What sin leads to that feeling of guilt? Name that as well and ask Jesus for forgiveness for it. If you've already confessed this sin, thank Jesus for forgiving it.

- "There is therefore now no condemnation for those who are in Christ Jesus" (Romans 8:1).

2. Examine the motives behind guilt in your life. Are you unwilling to be in God's debt? Are you seeking to justify yourself or earn God's favor? If so, admit this to your Lord and to yourself and receive the grace that frees your soul.

- "Sin will have no dominion over you, since you are not under law but under grace" (Romans 6:14).

3. Thank your Father for the blessing of his forgiveness. Ask his Spirit to help you see yourself as God sees you. And pray for the grace to forgive yourself as you are forgiven.

- "Blessed is the one whose transgression is forgiven, whose sin is covered" (Psalm 32:1).

GO

Our consumerist culture is built on performance and popularity. We are measured by what we do or by what we fail to do.

Because of that, every person you know who has not experienced the grace of God is struggling with the guilt of their sins and shortcomings. Perhaps they need to experience your forgiveness to believe in God's forgiveness. Or perhaps they simply need to know what you know: that grace is greater than guilt.

With whom will you share this liberating hope today?

Extended reading: Psalm 32

"Blessed is the one whose transgression is forgiven, whose sin is covered."

PSALM 32:1

SUNDAY

Join the "Fellowship of the Unashamed"

—

"He is not here, for he has risen, as he said." —Matthew 28:6

DAY 8

There is no natural explanation for the empty tomb of Christ.

The disciples could not have overpowered the Roman guards, nor could they have convinced more than five hundred eyewitnesses that a dead man was alive (1 Corinthians 15:6). And even if they somehow had, none would have died for something they knew to be a lie.

If the women had gone to the wrong tomb, the authorities would have corrected their error. If the authorities had stolen the body, they would have produced it. If Jesus did not die at the cross, that means he survived a spear thrust near his heart and three days in a mummified, air-tight burial shroud.

In his emaciated condition, he would have then had to shove aside the stone, appear through locked doors, and do the greatest high jump in history at the Ascension we see in Acts 1:9.

Easter is the foundation of the Christian faith. Because Jesus rose from the dead as he predicted, he must be divine. If he is divine, his words must be true. If he claimed to be our Savior and Lord, it must be so.

Now the risen king calls you and me to serve in his kingdom.

My favorite confession of faith was written in 1980 by an African Christian before he was martyred for his faith. I have quoted it often and am stirred each time by its words. Let's celebrate the resurrection of Jesus today by making its commitment our own:

> He said…
>
> I am part of the "Fellowship of the Unashamed." The die has been cast. I have stepped over the line. The decision has been made. I am a disciple of Jesus Christ. I won't look back, let up, slow down, back away, or be still. My past is redeemed, my present makes sense, and my future is secure. I am finished and done with low living, sight walking, small planning, smooth knees, colorless dreams, chintzy giving, and dwarfed goals.
>
> I no longer need preeminence, prosperity, position, promotions, plaudits, or popularity. I now live by presence, lean by faith, love by patience, lift by prayer, and labor by power. My pace is set, my gait is fast, my goal is heaven, my road is narrow, my way is rough, my companions few, my Guide reliable, my mission clear. I cannot be bought, compromised, deterred, lured away, turned back, diluted or delayed.

> I will not flinch in the face of sacrifice, hesitate in the presence of adversity, negotiate at the table of the enemy, ponder at the pool of popularity, or meander in the maze of mediocrity.
>
> I am a disciple of Jesus Christ. I must go until heaven returns, give until I drop, preach until all know, and work until he comes. And when he comes to get his own, he will have no problem recognizing me. My colors will be clear.

So as we enter our guided prayer today, may the same be true of us.

GUIDED PRAYER

1. Reflect on the miracle of Jesus' resurrection from the dead. Imagine the stone being rolled away and the risen Christ emerging from his tomb. Take a moment to worship him in the splendor of his resurrection glory.

- "When they saw him they worshiped him" (Matthew 28:17).

2. In one of his famous hymns, Charles Wesley wrote, "Christ the Lord is risen today, sons of men and angels say. Raise your joys and triumphs high; sing, ye heavens and earth reply." **What "joys and triumphs" can you claim because Jesus rose from the dead? How would you like to respond with gratitude to your risen Lord?**

- "Blessed be the God and Father of our Lord Jesus Christ! According to his great mercy, he has caused us to be born again to a living hope through the resurrection of Jesus Christ from the dead" (1 Peter 1:3).

3. Henry Wadsworth Longfellow wrote, "Twas Easter Sunday. The full-blossomed trees filled all the air with fragrance and with joy." **Give thanks to God for the new life and hope that is yours this day.**

- "Let your steadfast love, O Lord, be upon us, even as we hope in you" (Psalm 33:22).

GO

In *The Purpose Driven Life*, Rick Warren noted, "God specializes in giving people a fresh start." This "fresh start" began with Jesus' first disciples on Easter Sunday. On this day, they learned that their risen Lord would forgive their failures, abandonment, and betrayals leading to his death.

Their first impulse was to share with others the transforming grace they had received. This is still the best way you and I can celebrate the resurrection of Jesus. Secular people are often more open to spiritual truth at Christmas and Easter than at other times of the year. You have a strategic opportunity to explain the reason for your celebration today.

So as you go, pray by name for someone who needs the hope of Easter. Then ask God to help you be an answer to your prayer.

Extended reading: Matthew 28

Notes

Week 1

10   **only 5 percent of colonial Americans:** Library of Congress, *"Religion in Eighteenth-Century America - Religion and the Founding of the American Republic | Exhibitions (Library of Congress),"* www.loc.gov, June 4, 1998, https://www.loc.gov/exhibits/religion/rel02.html#:~:text=Between%201700%20and%201740%2C%20an,its%20first%20major%20religious%20revival.

13   **"Go home, lock yourself in your room":** Quoted in Stanley James Grenz, *Prayer: The Cry for the Kingdom* (United States: W.B. Eerdmans Publishing Company, 2005), 6.

16   **"One of the principal rules of religion":** John Wesley, *John and Charles Wesley: Selected Prayers, Hymns, Journal Notes, Sermons, Letters and Treatises* (United States: Paulist Press, 1981), 372.

20   *great people plant trees they'll never sit under:* Commonly attributed to Alfred North Whitehead but may be an adage that evolved over time. See "Blessed Are Those Who Plant Trees Under Whose Shade They Will Never Sit," Quote Investigator ˚, last modified April 29, 2020, https://quoteinvestigator.com/2020/04/29/tree-shade/.

23   **"To be loved but not known":** Tim Keller and Kathy Keller, *The Meaning of Marriage: Facing the Complexities of Commitment with the Wisdom of God* (United States: Penguin Publishing Group, 2013).

28   **"Another proof of the conquest of a soul":** Charles Spurgeon, The Complete Works of C. H. Spurgeon, *Volume 84* (N.p.: Delmarva Publications, Inc., 2015).

Week 2

39   **"Humility is not thinking less of yourself":** Rick Warren, *The Purpose Driven Life: What on Earth Am I Here For?* (Grand Rapids: Zondervan, 2007), 148.

47   **"practice the presence of God":** Brother Lawrence, *The Practice of the Presence of God* (United States: Baker Publishing Group, 1967).

51   **"Do all the good you can":** This precise phrasing has not been found in Wesley's works; however, sermons contain a partial match per "Do All the Good You Can; In All the Ways You Can," Quote Investigator, last modified September 24, 2016, https://quoteinvestigator.com/2016/09/24/all-good/

Week 3

60 **"the best and sweetest flowers of paradise"**: Thomas Brooks, *Smooth Stones Taken from Ancient Brooks: Being a Collection of Sentences, Illustrations, and Quaint Sayings, from the Works of that Renowned Puritan, Thomas Brooks* (United Kingdom: Sheldon, 1860).

62 **"The greatest tragedy of life is not unanswered prayer"**: Linda Star, *Are You the Result of Your Past? Be Careful with What Seeds You Allow to Take Root in the Garden of Your Heart* (United Kingdom: WestBow Press, 2017).

70 **George Mueller . . . . began praying for the conversion of five specific people**: Basil Miller, George Muller: *Man of Faith and Miracles* (Bloomington, MN: Bethany House Publishers, 1972), 146.

75 **Dwight Moody . . . "keep short accounts"**: Dwight Lyman Moody and Charles Frederic Goss, *Echoes from the Pulpit and Platform: Or, Living Truths for Head and Heart. Illustrated by Upwards of Five Hundred Thrilling Anecdotes and Incidents, Personal Experiences, Touching Home Scenes, and Stories of Tender Pathos Drawn from the Bright and Shady Sides of Life* (United States: A.D. Worthington, 1900), 617.

75 **"No man can do me a truer kindness"**: C. H. Spurgeon, *Sermons on Prayer* (United Kingdom: Marshall, Morgan & Scott, 1965).

79 **"More things are wrought by prayer than this world dreams of"**: Alfred Lord Tennyson, *Poems of Tennyson* (United States: Ginn, 1903), 216.

Week 4

93 **"The facts are that God is not silent"**: A. W. Tozer, *The Pursuit of God* (N.p.: Gideon House Books, 2017).

99 **"If we cooperate with him in loving obedience"**: A. W. Tozer, *The Pursuit of God* (N.p.: Gideon House Books, 2017).

101 **"I have been driven many times upon my knees"**: Attributed to Abraham Lincoln by Noah Brooks, *Harper's Weekly July 1865*. See also "Did Abraham Lincoln Actually Say That Obama Quote?," *Daily Beast*, last modified July 14, 2017, https://www.thedailybeast.com/did-abraham-lincoln-actually-say-that-obama-quote.

101 **"If we seek God for our own good and profit"**: Meister Eckhart, *The Westminster Collection of Christian Quotations* (United States: Westminster John Knox Press, 2001), 333.

101 **"Spiritual lust causes me to demand an answer from God"**: Oswald Chambers, *My Utmost for His Highest* (N.p.: Logos Research Systems, Incorporated, 2022).

102 **"Prayer is the way that the life of God in us is nourished"**: Oswald Chambers, *My Utmost for His Highest* (N.p.: Logos Research Systems, Incorporated, 2022).

107 **"The sacred promises, though in themselves most sure and precious"**: Charles Spurgeon, *The Complete Works of C. H. Spurgeon, Volume 34: Sermons 2001-2061* (N.p.: Delmarva Publications, Inc., 2015).

Week 5

118   **"When you've experienced grace and you feel like you've been forgiven":** Rick Warren, *quoted in Joseph A. Primm, Live the Journey (United States: Wipf and Stock Publishers, 2010).*

133   **"The old Puritans used to pray for 'the gift of tears'":** Oswald Chambers, *My Utmost for His Highest (N.p.: Logos Research Systems, Incorporated, 2022).*

135   **"To do so no more is the truest repentance":** Martin Luther, *The Westminster Collection of Christian Quotations (United States: Westminster John Knox Press, 2001).*

137   **"The next time the Lord speaks to you":** James S. Hewett, *Illustrations Unlimited (United States: Tyndale House Publishers, 1988), 216.*

Week 6

145   **Bob Buford's bestselling book:** Bob Buford, Halftime: *Changing Your Game Plan from Success to Significance (United States: Zondervan, 1997).*

150   **John MacDuff was right:** John MacDuff, *The Promised Land (United Kingdom: n.p., 1858).*

152   **starving children rescued from a Nazi concentration camp:** Matthew Dowling, "A Little Piece of Bread," Plymouth Church of Christ Blog, last modified August 21, 2020, https://www.plymouthcoc.net/content.cfm?id=151&blog_id=878.

157   **"How we spend our days":** Annie Dillard, *The Writing Life (United States: HarperCollins, 2009).*

161   **"Genuine Christian experience must always":** A. W. Tozer, *Men Who Met God: Twelve Life-Changing Encounters (United States: Moody Publishers, 2009).*

Week 7

176   **"God's mercies are new every morning. Receive them":** Max Lucado, *Every Day Deserves a Chance: Wake Up to the Gift of 24 Hours (United States: Thomas Nelson, 2007), 13.*

192   **"Grace teaches us that God loves because of who God is":** Philip Yancey, *What's So Amazing About Grace? (United States: Zondervan, 2008), 280.*

199   **I am part of the "Fellowship of the Unashamed":** The Gospel Truth, *"The Fellowship of the Unashamed,"* https://www.gospeltruth.net/unashamed.html

201   **"Twas Easter Sunday":** Henry Wadsworth Longfellow, *The Complete Poetical Works of Henry Wadsworth Longfellow (United Kingdom: Houghton, Mifflin, 1902), 33.*

201   **"God specializes in giving people a fresh start":** Rick Warren, *The Purpose Driven Life: What on Earth Am I Here For? (Grand Rapids: Zondervan,*

ABOUT DENISON MINISTRIES

—

Denison Ministries is a Christian nonprofit that seeks to transform the culture through Christ-centered content. The ministry accomplishes that through four distinct brands:

- **Denison Forum** (denisonforum.org) offers a biblical and redemptive perspective on current events through *The Daily Article* email newsletter and podcast, *The Denison Forum Podcast*, and many books and online resources.

- **Christian Parenting** (christianparenting.org) provides practical and spiritual resources, including an expansive podcast network, to help parents raise children to know and love the Lord.

- **First15** (first15.org) leads Christians into a transformative personal encounter with God through devotional readings, worship videos, and guided prayers.

- **Foundations with Janet** (foundationswithjanet.org) offers Bible study resources with blogs, videos, and biblical content for individual and small-group use.

Learn more at DenisonMinistries.org.

DENISON MINISTRIES